Murder, Poaching and Lemonade:
Crimes and court cases from nineteenth century West Lothian

Alex Adamson

Copyright © Alex Adamson, 2011
All rights reserved
ISBN-13: 978-1466353572
ISBN-10: 1466353570

Dedication:
I would like to thank to my wife Elinor, my mother, Harry, Ron, Sybil and Sheila for their help and support. They made many valuable suggestions and spotted errors as I developed the text. I would also like to thank Abigail for transforming the text into a book.

About the author:
Alex lives in Linlithgow with his wife and two children. He has been the Project Manager of the Buildings at Risk Register since 2007, first at the Scottish Civic Trust and since April 2011 at the Royal Commission on the Ancient and Historical Monuments of Scotland. He has an honours degree in History from Edinburgh University and a postgraduate diploma in European Urban Conservation from Dundee University.

Other books by the author:
   Linlithgow 1851: A Moment in Time
   Linlithgow - Architecture and History of a Scottish Royal Burgh - (Historical introduction by Alex Adamson, main text by Ron Smith), Linlithgow Civic Trust

Front cover:
Police photograph of Janet Walker (or Cunningham) of Linlithgow, convicted in 1880 of receiving stolen property. This picture, and that later in the book of John McLure, come from the 'Linlithgowshire Rogue's Gallery', a scrapbook of mug shots compiled by the Edinburgh Police over a period of around 30 years from the 1870s onwards. All images courtesy of Lothian and Borders Police and Edinburgh City Archives.

No part of this book may be reproduced or transmitted in any form or by any means, electronic, or mechanical, including photocopying, recording, without permission in writing from the author, except by a reviewer wishing to use short extracts in connection with a review.

Book design by Abigail Daly | abigaildaly@yahoo.co.uk

Contents

Introduction
    Crime Reporting   8
    Place and Personal Names   9
    Linlithgowshire in the Nineteenth Century   9
    Crime and Punishment in Nineteenth Century Britain   10
    The Legal System in Scotland   11

Chapter 1: 1801-1820 - The Early Days
    Introduction   14
    Mail Robberies   15
    Murder, Theft and Reward   17
    Theft from goods in transport   18
    Gang on the Run   23
    Unlawful Combination   25
    The Murderous Soldier   25
    The Highest Court in the Land   30
    Theft in the Early Nineteenth Century (1) – The Oatmeal Thief   32
    Theft in the Early Nineteenth Century (2) – Two Cases of House Breaking   34
    Respect for the Law   34
    Wanted – Reward Offered   35
    'Three Desperate Characters'   36

Chapter 2: 1821-40 – The World Gets Smaller
    Introduction   40
    Rape   41
    Theft in the 1820s   41
    A Crime Against the Elite - Two Cases of Poaching   42
    Multiple Fraud   44
    Assault and Robbery   45
    Incendiarism   46
    Attempted Highway Robbery   47

Financial Crime	48
A Day in the High Court in 1838	53
St Michael is Kinde to Strangers? – Assault and Robbery in Linlithgow	54
The Coming of the Railway – Tensions, Opportunities and Murder	55
The State of the (Criminal) Nation	63

Chapter 3: 1841-60 – Railway Mania and the Birth of the Shale Industry

Introduction	68
Domestic Violence	69
Part 1 - Death of a Child – May 1842	69
Part 2 - Culpable Homicide – July 1844	69
Part 3 - A Wicked Stepmother – May 1846	70
A Day in the High Court in 1842	71
Death in Custody	72
Injury in the Workplace, or Taking on the Dawsons (part 3)	74
Poaching in the 1840s and 50s	76
Alcohol, Public Houses and Public Order	77
Murder on the Canal	79
The Dangers of Rail Travel	80
The Upper Classes At Play – Part 1: Disorder in Linlithgow	81
The Upper Classes At Play – Part 2: Assault at Waverley Station	88
Beware – Card Sharks	91
Violent Assault	92
'Frightful Murder Near Bathgate' – Sectarian Violence in Linlithgowshire	92
McIver v McIver	98
Is No-one Safe?	99

Chapter 4: 1861-80 – The Height of Empire

Introduction	102
She Fought the Law and the Law Won	103
Absent Without Leave	104

'A Curious Case of Window-Breaking'	105
Clothes Theft	106
The Winchburgh Train Disaster	106
Part 1. The Crash	106
Part 2. The Search For Answers	108
Part 3. The Trial of Mr Latham and Mr Thomson	109
Part 4. Further Court Actions	111
Cattle Plague	115
Embezzlement	118
Toll Evasion	118
The Uphall Wife Killers	119
'Assault By a Jealous Shoemaker'	123
Breach of Promise	124
A Long Way From Home	125
'A Disorderly Town Councillor'	127
Infanticide	129
Complaints About the Court System	129
Impersonation and Theft	130
The Case That Never Was - 'The Right of Fishing in Linlithgow Loch'	132
Part 1 - A Call to Action	132
Part 2 - A Dash of Reality	133
Part 3 - A New Flashpoint	134
Part 4 - Peaceful Co-existence	135
Chapter 5: 1881-1900 – The End of the Century	
Introduction	138
Murder: Alleged and Attempted	139
Part 1 – Francis Kane and the Death of Mary Creely	139
Part 2 – A Most Respectable Man	140
Part 3 – The Death of Walter Russell	141
Frauds and Slanders	142

'An Elopement and its Consequences'	144
Bible Bashers	145
Birds of a Feather	145
Child Abuse	145
Part 1 – 'Alleged Inhumanity to Children By a Mother'	146
Part 2 – 'Shocking Cruelty'	146
Part 3 – 'Cruelty to Children'	147
The Evils of Alcohol	147
Assaulting a Police Officer	149
Health and Safety	150
'Soldiers Charged with Theft'	152
Poaching – Still a Serious Matter	152
Fraud	156
A Day in the Sheriff Court in 1897	157
'Contempt of Court'	159
Short and Sad	159
Lemonade Wars	160
Double Trouble	161
Endnotes	162
Postscript	163
Crimes and their punishments	165
Index	175

Introduction

Crime Reporting

Since newspapers began it has been found that crime stories sell copies. People can be fascinated, horrified or simply entertained by the scandals and wrong-doings of their fellows. We, today, share this impulse every bit as much as our Victorian forbears. In this book a selection of stories which span the period 1801 to 1900 are gathered together. With a few digressions, they mainly relate to the people and places of Linlithgowshire, the administrative area of the time which roughly corresponds to today's West Lothian. As well as the human interest in the people, and the crimes which they may, or may not, have committed, these stories help shed light on everyday life in a period when Linlithgowshire, along with the rest of Britain, was being transformed in many ways.

In the pages of this book are the accounts of many types of crime including thefts of various kinds, frauds, assaults, misdemeanours and a few murders. The people in the dock range from the desperate poor through to titled gentlemen. Some may be reviled, some pitied. The accounts are drawn from the newspapers of the time. Foremost among the sources are the Caledonian Mercury (an Edinburgh paper which ran from 1760 to 1867) and the Glasgow Herald (which is published today as the Herald). However, a wide range of newspapers and journals have been dipped into, where they have taken an interest in Linlithgowshire events. This takes us not just to other parts of Scotland but also to England, Ireland, the United States and even New Zealand (with its large Scottish ex-patriot population). Stories could be newsworthy for many reasons relating to their content, location, implications and the people involved, but it would be fair to say that those which travelled the furthest often had a novelty value to them.

With the exception of some socialist-leaning Chartist papers, these newspapers were generally read by the middle or upper classes and took a strongly pro-establishment line, especially on matters of law and order. At times, there is as much interest for us in the way a case has been reported as in the case itself.

The stories within these pages, of course, comprise only a small selection of the many cases related to West Lothian which occurred during the century. The most notorious cases are covered in depth, against a backdrop of the day-to-day activities of the courts. Over the course of the century we will see changes in the attitudes to crime and punishment.

Place and Personal Names

It is worth saying a brief word about the spelling of place names. Many of the locations which the journalists had to write about would have been unfamiliar to them, apart from which there was still a degree of flexibility about their spelling which the Ordnance Survey mapping of the country helped to eliminate from the 1850s onwards. Rather than attempt to correct or modernise the different spellings used in the articles I have followed the general rule of recording them in each story as the journalist wrote them. For some places, such as Borrowstounness (now almost universally known as Bo'ness) this has meant that a number of easily understandable variations appear.

A similar situation arises with proper names, especially for Irish surnames. Again, I have followed the spelling of the journalist rather than second-guessing any perceived errors.

Linlithgowshire in the Nineteenth Century

Linlithgowshire in 1800 was a predominantly agricultural county. There were a number of small towns including Bo'ness, Bathgate, Queensferry and Linlithgow, the county town which, with a population of around 2,500, was the largest.

Employment in the towns was dominated by traditional trades such as shoemaking (by far the biggest source of employment in Linlithgow itself), tanning, weaving, metal working, wood working and so on. The rural areas were dominated by agriculture, which brought a lot of people into the county. Many women were not formally employed, though those in rural areas would almost certainly be involved in farm work. Among those women who were salaried, working as a servant was the most common occupation, and was a way for many girls to start a new life away from home.

The course of the nineteenth century brought dramatic changes to Linlithgowshire, as it did to the rest of the country. The consequences of the Industrial Revolution, the Highland Clearances, the Irish Potato Famine and the dramatic developments in transport and communications all made their mark on the county. The greatest transformation took place in the south of the county where, from the middle of the century onwards, the shale oil industry created new towns and communities, and added thousands of new residents to the population. At the height of the boom, Linlithgowshire was the biggest oil producer in the world.

Across the county, the old trades were dying, out-competed by mass produced goods from other parts of the country. It was a slow, and sometimes painful, process. Handloom weavers were among the early victims of new technology and production methods. By the end of the century, only Linlithgow's shoemakers remained in any great numbers, and their time was limited. Agricultural improvements reduced the dependency on manual labour, which encouraged the drift from the countryside to the towns. By 1900 the majority of the population lived in towns.

This book is in no way intended to be a social history of the county, but in reading the court cases of the period one catches a glimpse, through the lives of individual people, of many of the changes which the community experienced.

Crime and Punishment in Nineteenth Century Britain

At the beginning of our period there were few jails of any size, and prisoners were expensive to guard and feed. Each county and burgh had its own prison, with the cost being borne by the local authority. In the case of Linlithgowshire it was situated in the Burgh Halls, or as it was then known the Town House or Tolbooth, until the middle of the century when a new building was constructed at the site now occupied by the court house. As time moves on, the court house is now being converted into a hotel with the judicial functions having been transferred to the new 'county town' – Livingston.

Mediaeval punishments such as mutilation were no longer in use, though there are records of whippings in the early years of the century and birching remained on the statute books for juveniles. Scots law allowed judges a flexibility in sentencing which was not present south of the border, and the standard tariffs were generally less severe than in England, where many offences carried the death penalty. Minor crimes could be dealt with by fines or short periods of incarceration, while more serious crimes attracted sentences of execution or banishment, which could be from the immediate locality, the county or the country. With the founding of Botany Bay in Australia in 1788 an additional option became available – transportation. In 1801, 493 male and 207 female convicts arrived in New South Wales, having survived journeys from England lasting around six to eight months. Not all were so lucky: 63 of their fellow prisoners died on route. Transportation sentencing was not highly nuanced. In most cases, the offender was given a tariff of seven years, and we will see that this was applied to a wide range of offences from the relatively trivial up to some which we would consider to be quite serious. Above that, lay sentences of ten, fourteen, or 21 years, and in the most extreme cases, transportation for life. The Scottish judicial system was somewhat slower than the English to embrace this alternative, with banishments still being handed out in the early years of the century. However, transportation soon became a standard punishment.

As each of the Australian colonies became better established they ceased to welcome convicts so new locations had to be found. After New South Wales, first Tasmania, then Norfolk Island, Victoria, Queensland and Western Australia became convict destinations. In 1840 Sydney successfully petitioned the crown to stop sending convicts. The final convict ship arrived in Australia in 1868. Over the course of this period around 162,000 people had been transported, of whom around 5% were thought to be Scots. By this time Britain had greatly expanded its prison system. Indeed, many of today's large Scottish prisons were founded in the last four decades of the century. Penal servitude was introduced as first an alternative, and then the replacement, to transportation. This involved hard labour such as the treadmill or the crank.

The Legal System in Scotland

During the nineteenth century, Scotland saw the development of a properly co-ordinated, professional police force. In the early years, much judicial power was devolved to local government. Burgh and Justice of the Peace Courts formed the lowest level in the system, dealing with minor misdemeanours. Where records survive from these courts they are not very detailed, often giving no more than the convicted person's name, crime and sentence. The next level up, and one which will occupy much of our attention, was the Sheriff Court, which operated at county level. Linlithgow Sheriff Court seems to have been a busy place throughout our century. This was typically a multi-stage process, with the Sheriff, or his substitute, examining the accused and key witnesses before proceeding to a full trial where there seemed to be a case to answer. Sometimes proceedings were delayed pending further investigation into the people involved or the circumstances of the alleged offence.

More serious cases would go to the High Court of Justiciary, in Edinburgh. This court still exists today, but is usually known simply as the High Court. The only higher court in Scotland was the Court of Session. Beyond that, in these pre-European Union times, the only court of appeal was the House of Lords, which Linlithgow cases reached on a few, rare occasions.

Chapter 1:
1801-1820: The Early Days

The Early Years

Introduction

The eighteenth century had been a turbulent period for the people of Scotland. It had seen the departure of the Parliament from Edinburgh to Westminster in 1707, the end of Stuart rule and the establishment of the Hanoverian dynasty in 1714, the unsuccessful Jacobite risings of 1715 and '45, the loss of the American colonies in 1783, the French Revolution of 1789 and subsequent wars with France, which would carry on until the final defeat of Napoleon in 1815.

The closure of many European ports during much of the first two decades of the century was to have a serious impact on the British economy, yet this was also a time of great innovation, first in agriculture and then in industry. It is towards the end of the eighteenth century that the first, great, mechanised mills were constructed at places such as New Lanark. Nearer to West Lothian, the Carron Ironworks opened its doors in 1759, and by 1814 it was the largest such works of its kind in Europe, employing more than 2,000 workers. Though West Lothian was not the setting for major developments at this time, they would have had an increasing effect on the lives of its inhabitants.

One of the features of the cases in this chapter is that movement of goods and people into, or across, West Lothian was a slow process. The County was remote to the big cities of the Central Belt in a way which it is difficult to imagine today.

Responsibility for the custody of prisons lay with Scotland's many burghs. In the 1780s a number of them had been visited by the great English prison reformer John Howard. He had found them to be *'old buildings, dirty and offensive, without courtyards and generally without water.'* The sexes were mixed, prison keepers sold alcohol to the inmates, and infection and illness were rife. Despite all that, he thought that they were of a better standard than their English and continental counterparts!

THE EARLY YEARS

Mail Robberies
Sources:
Caledonian Mercury, Thursday 5th August 1802
Aberdeen Journal, Wednesday 23rd March 1803

In the early days of the nineteenth century travel and communication were far slower than today. Roads were very poor and journeys that we could make today by road or train in a matter of hours took days. Undaunted, regular mail services were being set up round the country. In Scotland, one of the most significant routes was that between Edinburgh and Glasgow. The mail was carried by horse, and part of the journey took it through Linlithgowshire. A crime committed on Sunday 1st August 1802 was to have an effect on the way mail was transported throughout Scotland.

Sabbath or not, when news reached Edinburgh that the post had been robbed three miles from Linlithgow, the authorities sprang into action. Three officials of the General Post Office, Mr Ker (secretary), Mr Beveridge (solicitor) and Mr Ronaldson (surveyor) immediately set to work on the capture of the perpetrators. With the support of the city magistrates and the Sheriff, they sent messengers off in various directions to alert the authorities in neighbouring areas.

In fact, those responsible for the robbery were not fleeing the area. Instead, they decided to go into Edinburgh and make the most of their ill-gotten gains. On Monday, the very next day, word came through to the postal officials that two suspicious persons had arrived in the town the previous evening. The men's behaviour continued to draw attention to them and on Tuesday the order went out for their apprehension. The two men tried to hide but were tracked down to separate addresses in Rose Street. One of them nearly managed to evade capture by the cunning trick of hiding on a bed under a pile of dirty washing!

That afternoon they were examined by the Sheriff, who obtained a full confession from them. He discovered that their names were Robert Brown and James Clark (a.k.a. Stewart), and that both were army deserters. In their possession they were found to have notes to the value of £60 – a fortune for the time. One of them even had a £20 note!

Naturally, the authorities were keen to recover as much of the stolen property as possible. On Wednesday, Brown, two clerks of the Post Office and two Sheriff's officers, went in chaises to a wooded hill near Linlithgow where the villain showed his captors the surviving evidence of the crime. He took them to a large

The Early Years

stone, under which there was a hole. In the hole were the remains of the letters and packages, which they had set fire to after removing the valuables.

The newspaper report concluded with somewhat self-congratulatory comments on the law and order system in Edinburgh:

'We have had frequent occasion to notice the propriety with which the policy [meaning 'policing'] of this city is conducted. It is seldom that street robberies, or other such heinous offences, are perpetrated here; but when they do occur a few days generally secure the culprits. Probably no city of its magnitude has ever evinced a greater degree of vigilance; and the present instance, where the mail robbers, who took refuge in it, have been so speedily apprehended, is a strong proof of the justice of the remark. The Magistrates and the Sheriff are well entitled to the gratitude of the citizens for the peace and protection which they enjoy.'

So how did this incident change the postal system? The concern it generated led to the following announcement in the same edition of the Caledonian Mercury:

'NEW MAIL TO GLASGOW
The Banks, Bankers, and principal Merchants of this city, have applied to the Post Master General for a mail coach to run betwixt Edinburgh and Glasgow, which we doubt not, will be set a-going, being so much for the interest and safety of the revenue and the public. The recent robbery of the mail near Linlithgow, which was carried on horseback, makes this more necessary.'

This was a logical step to take, building on the success of the London to Edinburgh service, which had been introduced in 1786. In time, mail coaches were established on many Scottish routes. They carried people as well as mail and made a significant contribution to communications around the country.

Just seven months later another postal crime was recorded in Linlithgowshire. It was one of two crimes with references to the county among those tried at the High Court of Justiciary in Edinburgh on Saturday 19th March 1803.

John Berry was accused of taking letters out of bags being sent from Borrowstounness to Linlithgow. He confessed his guilt and was banished from Scotland for seven years. Less lucky was James Taylor, from Linlithgow. He was accused of what sounds like a less serious crime: stealing butter and cheese. Having pled guilty he was sentenced to be banished from Scotland for life.

THE EARLY YEARS

A case reported the same day as James Taylor's shows that the human life, or at least that of a poor person, was not held so dear as the letters, butter or cheese. Glasgow magistrates tried Mrs Kilpatrick and Widow Henderson for shutting their doors against one of their lodgers, a girl called Mary Brounlie. Mary was suffering from a fever and, too ill to find alternative accommodation, died on their doorstep. The women's defence was that they were not related to the deceased and had given her lodgings for some time merely from a sense of charity. When they had realised that she did not have long to live they had decided to get rid of her, so as not to be landed with the expense of her funeral, which they could ill afford. Mrs Kilpatrick was imprisoned for one month and fined two guineas. Mrs Henderson was banished from the city for three years.

Murder, Theft and Reward
Source:
Caledonian Mercury, Monday 13th July 1807
Aberdeen Journal, Wednesday 22nd July 1807 and Wednesday 29th July 1807

Violent crime was every bit as serious an issue in the nineteenth century as it is today. Through the course of this book, we will see a number of cases of assault, homicide and murder. When a violent act resulted in the death of the victim, one of the difficult decisions that faced a jury was whether or not the accused had intended to kill or if it was, to some degree, unintentional.

A case of this type was that of Richard Hamilton, which came before the High Court of Justiciary on Saturday 11th July 1807. Hamilton was accused of hamesucken and murder. Hamesucken is a term in Scots Law which means to break into someone's house with the intent of seriously assaulting them, and then carrying out the attack.

Hamilton had been living in Grangepans (now part of Bo'ness) and working as a miner. The offence of which he was accused had been committed almost ten years earlier. One of Hamilton's near neighbours was an old, infirm widow called Katherine Stewart. Her husband, James, had also been a miner but had died some time before. Something happened between Hamilton and Katherine Stewart – quite what, the records do not show, but the result was that on 7th August 1797 Hamilton approached her house in a violent temper. He broke down the door and beat her severely. He ran from the scene and Katherine was found, still alive, but fatally injured, with bruising to her head, neck and other parts of the body. She survived for some hours before passing away the next day.

The Early Years

Possibly having heard of her death, Hamilton fled the locality and was not caught until October 1806.

The jury found him guilty of hamesucken, which seems to have been clear cut, but found it harder to establish whether he had meant to kill of just to injure Widow Stewart. Only a minority thought that he had set out to commit murder and eventually they reached agreement, finding him guilty of the lesser (but still serious) crime of culpable homicide. After considering the matter for a week, the court sentenced him to be transported overseas for life.

In the case of the postal robbery in 1802 we saw a Caledonian Mercury journalist express great satisfaction with the powers of law enforcement in Edinburgh. The case of Richard Hamilton shows that justice could be evaded, sometimes for years, by the simple act of going to a different part of the country where you were not known. Clearly, the officers of the law were, at times, in need of assistance. The following article, printed in the Caledonian Mercury for Monday 13th July, the same day in which it reported Hamilton's trial, shows that crime fighting in Linlithgowshire was not simply left to the authorities:

'At the General Annual Meeting of the Delegates of the different parishes in the county of Linlithgow, associated for the purpose of prosecuting thieves, &c. held at Linlithgow on the 19th June last, the meeting unanimously voted the sum of five guineas from their funds to Mr WILLIAM GLENDINNING, tenant at Livingstone Mill, in the parish of Livingstone (although no-wise connected with the Society), as a reward for his great exertions in apprehending and bringing to justice Thomas Smith, horse-breaker at Newcastle, and George Stevenson, cabinet-maker there, both some time ago executed in consequence of a sentence of the High Court of Justiciary, for stealing a horse belonging to Mr GLENDINNING, and two others, the property of the Rev. Mr ROBERTSON, minister of Livingstone. And the said sum has been paid to Mr GLENDINNING accordingly.'

Theft From Goods in Transport
Source:
Caledonian Mercury, Monday 23rd May 1808, Monday 1st July 1811, Thursday 18th July 1811 and Saturday 20th July 1811

As noted in the introduction, Linlithgow in the nineteenth century was a town of trade and small scale manufacturing. One of the larger businesses was the distillery, first sited at Bonnytoun and later relocated (in 1834) to the canal-side

The Early Years

site at St Magdalene's (which had been operating as a distillery since the late eighteenth century). The distillery was the foundation of the wealth of one of the most powerful families in the town during the century – the Dawsons. They were no-nonsense businessmen who were always ready to defend their own interests. The patriarch of the dynasty was Adam Dawson. In 1811 he was to become provost, a post that he would hold until 1818. Indeed, from 1811 to 1881 a Dawson would be provost for 51 of the 70 years.

In 1808 Adam Dawson uncovered a conspiracy to defraud him and sought justice in the courts. The resulting trial was held in the Sheriff Court on 15th May 1808. It is noteworthy how many people had been involved in the crime.

The distillery, of course, needed grain. Some of the grain used at Bonnytoun was shipped to Bo'ness where it passed through the hands of John Grierson, grain measurer. He verified the quantity delivered, stored it in his warehouse and then transferred it by cart to the distillery. For the measurements to be slightly out from time-to-time might have been understandable, but Grierson was found guilty of stealing a share from a number of cargos and reselling it for his own profit. A number of local carters were charged with collusion in these crimes: James Galbreath, Janet Cowie, William Brown, John Glass, Walter Pollock, John Meikle, Thomas Carlaw and Peter Henderson. With the exception of Meikle all were found guilty. Grierson was sentenced to be imprisoned in the jail in Linlithgow for one month and only to be released after that period on payment of a fine of £10 (equivalent to around £5,000 - £6,000 at 2011 prices). The guilty carters got one week in prison and a fine of two guineas. The men (and woman) were immediately transferred to the jail for the commencement of their sentences.

The transportation of goods continued to give rise to crime: the length of time that journeys took cannot have helped. Shipments between Edinburgh and Glasgow that would later take under a day by canal, then later still just a few hours by train, took two or three days in the first decades of the century, or longer if the roads were not passable. Linlithgowshire was handily placed for an overnight stop for carters between the two cities, as a result of which it became the setting for some of the key scenes in the trial of James Hamilton at the High Court of Justiciary in 1811. This case illustrates the carting process and the opportunities for misappropriating goods. Though only one man was in the dock on this occasion, the evidence suggests that many people were involved, and at least one more came to trial. The charges related to *'stealing and pilfering from the carts of the Glasgow and Edinburgh carriers'* and related to a number of incidents

The Early Years

over a six month period.

The accused was an inn-keeper at Dechmont Park, near Uphall. After his arrest, he was held in the tolbooth of Linlithgow until his trial. Adam Tough, a carter from Glasgow (held in prison in Glasgow) would later face trial for his actions.

The case arose following complaints by a Glasgow business man called James Aitken, who regularly transported goods to and from Glasgow. Aitken kept detailed books in which he recorded all his business transactions: goods received and sent out, dates and amounts etc. Every load went out with a way-bill, which was handed over to the recipient, allowing him to check that what was delivered matched what was dispatched. It was a comprehensive system which did not allow much scope for fraud, as the accused were to find out.

On 29th November 1810 Mr Aitken had dispatched, among other things, three puncheons of rum to Messers John Durie & Co., of Leith. A puncheon was twice the size of a standard barrel and would typically hold 72 gallons. Now, Aitken had a number of men working for him at that time but the two who were entrusted with taking the carts through to Leith were David Gray and Daniel McLellan. This seemed like a routine delivery: Aitken was very used to transporting goods between Glasgow and Edinburgh and there was a set routine. Once loaded up, his carts would leave Glasgow between eight and eleven in the morning. The distance to Edinburgh meant that a journey there would involve two overnight stops, arriving on the third day. As scheduled, the rum was delivered on 2nd December – so far, so good – but the trouble began when it was measured out, in the presence of Aitken's Edinburgh agent, by the principal porter at Durie & Co. The order was undeniably two gallons short of the amount entered on the way-bill. Though this was a small percentage of the total, it was a valuable amount of spirits in itself. John Durie himself was summoned and the three men examined the casks, but they couldn't find any leaks or reasonable explanation for the shortfall. Durie was most unhappy and eventually agreed to pay, but insisted that if another delivery arrived short he would not be doing so again. Not surprisingly, he followed up with a letter of complaint to Aitken, which arrived a few days later. It is fascinating to see how events which today would take perhaps a couple of hours took the best part of a week in 1810.

Aitken, of course, was furious. This was not the first time he had had complaints and for the good of his business he knew that something needed to be done. He questioned Gray and McLellan about the rum but they denied taking any, or any knowledge of what had happened to the missing gallons. Next, Aitken approached a local magistrate, suggesting that the men be asked to swear an oath that they had not stolen it. The magistrate, however, laughed at the idea that a carter's oath was of any value, but agreed to investigate the case.

During the course of the enquiries, and the court case that followed, the key questions were answered and a picture was pieced together of the events which had occurred between the departure of the rum from Aitken's yard on 29th November and the arrival of most of it in Leith on 2nd December.

Daniel McLellan and David Gray had set off with two cartloads of rum. McLellan was new to the business, having only started working for Aitken the week before, and this was his first trip. Gray was more experienced and seems to have been mentoring him. McLellan had the cartload for Durie & Co., while Gray had an identical consignment, destined for the Navy. As both loads were for Edinburgh this must have seemed like an ideal chance to let someone show McLellan the ropes. McLellan seems to have been a fairly naive sort of man and Aitken clearly hadn't allowed for the way in which he could be led and taken advantage of.

On the first day, they travelled as far as Airdrie without incident. The next day they set off at about eight or nine in the morning, stopping at Jenny Bauchop's public house for a quarter of an hour to water the horses. It was here that the impropriety seems to have begun. McLellan saw Gray coming away from the carts with a jug full of rum and a gimlet (a type of drill), though he wasn't sure which cart the rum might have come from. Later that day they stopped in at the Armadale Inn, where they met two other carters, James Watt and John Lothian. At about three o'clock, the four of them left for James Hamilton's inn at Dechmont Park. The journey was about seven and a half miles and took them three hours. The speed of travel, combined with the need to refresh the horses (and the men), helps explain why the whole journey took three days. Even this short stretch of the trip was broken by a brief stop at Mrs Ainslie's public house, on the west side of Bathgate.

It was at Dechmont that that key events of the case took place. Gray, Watt, Lothian and Hamilton seemed to be acting as if by pre-arrangement. Hamilton was waiting for them with a candle, which he held up while one of the other men drilled a hole in one of McLellan's casks (using Hamilton's gimlet). Hamilton then held a large, white iron can under the cask until it was full of rum. While he carried it into the inn, Gray filled a second smaller one. The cask was then stopped up by a pin which someone had to hand. Slow though he was, McLellan had a feeling that this wasn't right, and he asked the others what was going on.

The Early Years

They told him that it was fine, and that Hamilton had paid 5s a pint for it. They assured him that it was well understood that the carters were allowed to *'tak a drap'* at Dechmont Park, and indeed that they were permitted to help themselves to dram from the cask if the weather was wet, or cold or just when they felt they needed it! They poured out a draught for McLellan and treated him with great camaraderie.

The next day, they arrived in Leith and the reception they received began to make it clear to McLellan that all was not well. On their return to Glasgow they were brought before Mr Aitken. Gray denied everything and McLellan seems to have thought it best to take the same line. Though clearly not without suspicions, Aitken had decided to believe them – after all, the rum could have been stolen without their knowledge – and he kept McLellan and Gray in his employment. Emboldened, Gray seems to have seen this as the green light to carry on creaming off a share of the goods in his charge. On 20th February 1811 McLellan and Gray were again spending the night at Hamilton's inn, this time carrying a cargo of ink and clothing, from which Hamilton took two shirts and a pair of grey breeches or pantaloons - an event attested by a number of witnesses. On a third trip, in March, they had been transporting three boxes of tea. He, Gray and Hamilton had broken into the boxes and removed as much tea as Hamilton could pay for at 5s a pound. What Hamilton couldn't afford, Gray then sold to Mrs Forrester in Bathgate.

This testimony was not good for Hamilton and there was further bad news for him when one of his neighbours gave evidence of another theft committed the previous November. Calling in *'about breakfast time to get a dram'*(!) this man saw tea being taken from a cart driven by Adam Tough (like the previously mentioned James Watt, he was a servant of Mr William Stewart of Edinburgh). The neighbour recalled a disagreement between Hamilton and Tough after which Hamilton damned him, and said he would be hanged for stealing yet.

A rather comical, if somewhat desperate, incident seems to have occurred at this stage of the trial with the defence counsel, Mr Murray, objecting to the charge relating to this particular incident, which specified that the theft was from goods under the control of Adam Tough. He argued that the charge was not valid because Mr Stewart's servant's name was in fact Abraham, not Adam. Tough's mother was called to give evidence and confirmed that he was called Abraham, but the bail application he had signed (he now being held in prison in Glasgow) was signed Adam, demonstrating that he used both names.

From all these accounts it would seem that a very strong case had been made against James Hamilton. However, class mattered and Hamilton was a cut above mere carters. His defence counsel, argued that his client was the victim of a conspiracy by the carters to have him found guilty of crimes which they themselves had committed. Certainly, the evidence given by the carters seems to have raised many questions and to confirm the prejudices of the magistrates that dishonesty was rife amongst this profession. Three local farmers, Alexander Hill, Mr White and John Smith, were called by the defence, all of whom bore testament to his good character, before the counsels summed up. Mr Murray seems to have done his job well, raising so many doubts that the jury were not able to agree on Hamilton's guilt, though not willing to find him innocent either. In the end they reached that classic Scottish compromise of Not Proven. The judge clearly had his doubts about how clean Hamilton's hands were in these matters. It was noted that he only released Hamilton after an impressive admonition.

Gang on the Run
Source:
The Examiner, Sunday 1st January 1815
Caledonian Mercury, Monday 23rd January 1815, Thursday 15th June 1815, Thursday 29th June 1815 and Saturday 15th July 1815

The Examiner, a London Sunday paper, reported an exciting, if somewhat grizzly, incident from Linlithgow prison. Though this was an interesting story in itself it formed one part of a longer story which unfolded over a number of months from late 1814 to the middle of 1815.

In October of the preceding year, John Grant, known as Brosie, and a number of other Grangepans residents (miners Thomas Frew senior and junior amongst them) had been accused of assaulting and robbing travelling merchant Charles McBrierty. They were arrested soon after and held pending trial. On 1st November the Frew clan somehow managed to escape, leaving Grant behind in Linlithgow Prison, which it must be remembered was in part of the Tolbooth (now the Burgh Halls), standing between the High Street and the Palace. On 20th December Grant saw a chance and also made a break for it. The alarm was raised immediately and he was pursued by a number of people, some on foot and some on horseback. Finding himself hemmed in and likely to be recaptured he fled in the only direction open to him – north towards Linlithgow Loch. He plunged into what must have been freezing water and managed to swim almost to the

The Early Years

far side. Meanwhile, his pursuers raced round the sides of the Loch, intent on apprehending him wherever he might appear. With the far bank in sight, Grant saw that escape was impossible. The onlookers reported that he sank, never to rise again. Eleven days later, when the report was written, the body had still not been found.

The events surrounding the rest of the gang were reported in a number of articles in the Caledonian Mercury, and other titles. The Frew clan consisted of Thomas Frew senior, a miner aged about 70, his son Thomas Frew junior, his grandson Alexander Cuming (illegitimate son of his daughter Elizabeth) and Thomas junior's wife, Jean Anderson. Following their escape, the Linlithgowshire Justices of the Peace offered a reward of ten guineas to anyone who delivered one of the Frews to a Scottish jail, to which the Magistrates of the burgh of Linlithgow offered an additional ten guineas reward for the capture of Thomas junior. The rewards were published in the national press and just over two months later, on January 16th, the whole gang was apprehended in Hamilton.

On Saturday 21st January, they were escorted to Linlithgow by a group of special constables (senior men from the burgh of Linlithgow) aided by full time soldiers attached to the local militia. It must have been quite a sight! Arriving late in the day, they were immediately brought before a packed court and remanded in custody. Jean seems to have been released fairly quickly and the three men were held in Linlithgow jail for the best part of four months before being transferred to the tolbooth in Edinburgh on 12th June, ahead of a trial at the High Court of Justiciary the following month.

Despite all the excitement and drama of the build up, when the case was finally heard it proved to be something of a damp squib. Thomas senior pled guilty, as did his grandson, Alexander Cuming. Thomas junior pled not guilty and after a few witnesses had been heard it became clear that there was insufficient evidence to gain a conviction against him. The public prosecutor therefore gave up the case and he was set free.

When it came to sentencing, the defence counsel, Mr Jeffrey, asked for the ages of the guilty men to be taken into account. The court appears to have been relatively lenient, for the times, sending Thomas senior to Bridewell prison, and transporting Alexander overseas for seven years.

Unlawful Combination
Source:
Caledonian Mercury, Monday 6th February 1815

The industrial revolution brought about many changes in British society. In the early decades, the businessmen had the upper hand, and there were very few laws to protect workers. Hours were long, health and safety were unknown and women and children were employed as cheap labour. Over time, the workers began to try to organise themselves in order to negotiate collectively with their employers. Out of this activity, the trade union movement was to emerge. Many businessmen realised that this posed a threat to the unfettered power they had over their workforce and used their influence to have the forming of unions, or combinations, as they were known, made illegal. With the spectre of revolutionary France hanging over the British elite, they argued that more was at stake than just their profits.

A local case from 1815 shows that it was not just in the big, new industrial cities that such ideas were fermenting. One of the largest single employers in Linlithgow in the early years of the nineteenth century was the calico print works on the River Avon. Calico was a type of linen textile.

'This day the High Court of Justiciary met, when the diet was called against James Miller, and George Paterson, calico printers at Avon printfield, accused of unlawful combination. Neither of them appearing, sentence of fugitation was pronounced against them. William Burns, calico printer, at Levenfield, accused of the same crime, also failing to appear, was likewise outlawed.'

In other words, Miller, Paterson and Burns were declared to be fugitives from the law, or outlaws. We will see that as late as 1840 this was far from rare.

The Murderous Soldier
Source:
Caledonian Mercury, Saturday 28th January 1815, Monday 6th February 1815 and Thursday 23rd February 1815

James Murdoch was a young man, reckoned to be about 23 years old, who earned his living as a grocer in Langrighead, in the parish of Whitburn. From the testimony of some of his neighbours who knew him well it seems that he was a

The Early Years

very decent and much respected man. He lived in a small house comprising a bed/living room, a room for the shop and a coal cellar.

The story of his murder, and the High Court trial of his unrelated namesake, John Murdoch, caused considerable interest in the press, with a wealth of detail being reported. Though murder was obviously the most serious element, John was also charged with stealing James' silver watch, a one pound note of the Stirling Banking Company, four shillings in silver, and three handkerchiefs, all of which were found in his possession when he was apprehended.

Children grew up a lot earlier in the nineteenth century. By the time he was twenty, John Murdoch had already completed an apprenticeship as a wright, worked for a year as a journeyman in that trade, joined the army, served in the artillery in Spain, been wounded in the Battle of Vitoria[1] and pensioned out of the service. Early in the January 1815 he visited James Murdoch, an old acquaintance. Indeed, we know that John had spent part of the previous summer with him in Langrighead, during which time he had become known to a number of the locals. On the current occasion he had been staying there for a few days when their friendship turned violent. James, and presumably John, spent the evening of 24th January in Greenhorn's inn without any sign of impending trouble: the next day James was brutally killed.

Other than John Murdoch, the last person to see James alive seems to have been John Lindsay, a boy aged about twelve or thirteen. He was the son of a farmer from nearby Langrig. He called at the house at half past eight on the morning of 25th January to buy a halfpenny worth of ink. He had expected the shop to be open but found the door barred. He knocked, and heard James rise and move about inside. Eventually the door was opened, Lindsay explained what he wanted and James fetched the ink. While he was waiting for his purchase, Lindsay saw John Murdoch in the bedroom.

Having taken the ink home, Lindsay next passed the shop half an hour or so later on his way to school. Standing outside at this time was another would-be customer, John Geddes, who had walked half a mile from his father's farm to buy tobacco. Geddes, too, was surprised to find the windows and doors shut up at that hour of the morning. He knew that James was a little deaf so he tried banging and shaking the door, but got no response. He was later to tell the court that he had told a passing acquaintance that: *'Murdoch is dead, or something worse!'* However, like many who like to claim wisdom after the event, he doesn't seem to have taken his own prophecy seriously enough to take any action.

THE EARLY YEARS

A few other people tried and failed to get an answer at the door that morning but it was not until late afternoon that the people of Langrighead became seriously concerned by the lack of activity in the house.

At about five pm, a few friends and acquaintances of James Murdoch fell into conversation outside the shop. James Forrest was a local labourer and a friend of James Murdoch, and had been with him in Greenhorn's the previous night. Thomas Dunlop, like Geddes, had tried to get into the shop between nine and ten in the morning. Finding it shut, he had got on with his daily business, which had taken him to Bathgate. Dunlop had returned to the shop in the hope of buying the snuff he had been looking for in the morning. Forrest and Dunlop found it highly suspicious that the house was still shut up and decided to try and get in. They found that the door was barred (from the inside) but not locked. There must have been something of a gap between the door and the door case because they reckoned, rightly, that they could cut through the bar. They roped in a couple of extra men, John Robb and William Black to help them. Robb was a useful recruit because he had a saw close at hand with which he was able to cut through the bar, allowing the four men to get into the house.

The first thing they saw was John Murdoch walking softly across the room. *'Is that you, John?'* Forrest asked him. John said he was feeling badly, and had been in bed all day. He must have planned this cunning story since, as if to corroborate it, he was wearing a night cap on his head, even though he was fully dressed! Forrest asked him where James was and was told that he had gone to Bathgate and hadn't returned yet. Forrest noticed that there was no fire in the grate and offered to light one, to help keep John warm. John refused the offer and said he wanted to go back to bed. He tried to get the men to leave. The men were looking around, trying to work out what was going on. In a panic, John told them that James had left orders that no-one was to go into the shop because all the goods were lying out. More suspicious than ever, Forrest again tried to engage John on the subject of lighting a fire, distracting him by gathering up coals while subtly winking to Barr to slip into the shop. Sneaking in through a back passage, Robb saw the victim lying on his back, dead. He was moved to exclaim, *'The conscience is bad!'* On hearing this, Murdoch tried to make a run for it, quickly pursued by the four men, who followed crying out, *'There is a murderer here!'* John got out of the house and was running along the side of it when he was caught by Black and a passerby.

The men took John Murdoch to the back of the house and searched him, finding five handkerchiefs, two sealed parcels, four shillings, James Murdoch's penknife

The Early Years

and a shoemaker's awl. For some reason they then shifted him to the smiddy and searched him again. Strapped to his right leg they found a package containing eight pounds and a shilling in notes and one pound and eighteen shilling in silver (of which three shillings and sixpence were *'bad'* or forged). In his pockets they found James Murdoch's watch. John protested that the money was his own, but wasn't so foolish as to claim the other items. Having had the presence of mind to make an inventory of what they had found, the men decided to send Forrest off to find Major Shillinglaw, the nearest justice. Shillinglaw told them to take the prisoner to the Sheriff in Whitburn and promised to follow on behind on horseback. What were the men to do with the items they had found? In a move which seems to have been seen as sensible to the court but which would cause uproar today, they divided them between themselves and took them home! Indeed, Forrest was to be particularly praised in the court for his actions during the affair. The Lord Justice Clerk[2] commended him, saying that his conduct *'would have been an honour to the first officer of police.'* Praise indeed!

Two medical men, James Weir and Robert Purdie, were called over from Linlithgow to examine the body. They found the scene to be *'awash with blood, and a little brain'.* James Murdoch had received three crashing blows to the head, probably delivered by the blood splattered adze (a type of axe) found at the scene. Weir reported that any one of these wounds would have proved fatal: all three had broken through the skull, leaving wounds about an inch in diameter through which the brains were seeping. For good measure, John had strangled James, tying a silk handkerchief round his neck and twisting it so tightly that it had to be cut off with a knife.

A few days later they marched him through the snow to the Sheriff-Substitute in Linlithgow, a distance of thirteen miles. Murdoch complained that he had a fever, but got little sympathy. After a short spell in prison there it was decided that he was to be transported under guard to Edinburgh and, because of the danger he was seen to pose, kept in *'the cage'* for nearly three weeks in advance of his trial.

Of course, it would be unfair not to relate John Murdoch's account of the events. Yes, he had been found in very suspicious circumstances, but that did not mean that he was necessarily guilty. His defence hinged on a new character to the drama: a Glasgow spoonmaker called John Brown. According to Murdoch, Brown had come to the shop and quarrelled with James Murdoch about some money which Brown owed him. Brown then struck James on the head with John's adze, killing him. Apparently, Brown's next move was to plant the various items belonging to James Murdoch on John Murdoch's person. Hearing people

The Early Years

knocking on the door, Brown climbed out of a window saying that he would return that night. For reasons he was not able to explain, Murdoch had chosen to spend the rest of the day in the house, and he did not dispute the details of his capture.

Dubious though this account sounded, the court called John Brown to give evidence. He stated, bluntly, that never in his life had he been to Langrighead, Whitburn or at any other part of the county, except in coming to attend this trial. He had been apprehended in Glasgow and examined, during which he was able to prove that he had been in Glasgow during the whole of January. He had met John Murdoch, in Glasgow, on New Year's Day but had never met or heard of James Murdoch. Brown's employer, James Noval, combmaker, was able to confirm his alibi, in fact he particularly remembered giving Brown work on the day of the murder, the 25th of January.

John asked to be allowed to amend his account, as he realised that it was erroneous in a number of the details! His new, Brown-free, account began on the night before the murder. James and John had spent a pleasant couple of hours playing pitch and toss, and had gone to bed on very friendly terms. The next morning, after Lindsay had called for his ink, they had resumed the game. Unfortunately, they soon began to quarrel and James struck John. Being thus provoked, John hit back, striking James on the head with an adze, and repeated the blow twice more as he lay on the ground, and afterwards twisted a small stick into the napkin that was round Murdoch's neck. Immediately afterwards, he took the watch and other articles mentioned in the indictment. Following the murder, feeling a fever coming on, he fastened the door and went to bed.

Though he had pled not guilty, this was a confession, and the jury, not surprisingly, returned a unanimous guilty verdict. The five judges each took turns to sum up. They were appalled at the violent nature of the crime and the abuse of hospitality. The Lord Justice Clerk, having touched on these aspects, went on to talk about Murdoch's status as an ex-soldier:

'You, Sir, are the first person, since this country was favoured with the blessings of peace[3], who having been engaged in actual service, and the defence of your country, have appeared at this bar, accused of any crime; you have brought a disgrace on your honourable profession, to suppose one moment, that because you are a soldier, you had therefore liberty to commit murder, or any other crime. This idea will, I am confident, be detested by every honourable soldier or sailor. They are selected as the guardians of their country, and when, having fought its battles, they return to their

The Early Years

families, and the bosoms of their friends, they return with their well-earned pension which the country gives to their merits, to act with the honest and virtuous dignity of soldiers in their private situations, and to act as men who revere the law. You, sir, have unhappily betrayed that depravity of heart which you fostered and are, therefore, to be exhibited to society, as a lasting monument of the awful effects of sin.'

The Duke of Wellington seems to have had a somewhat less romantic view of the troops: 'Ours [our army] is composed of the scum of the earth – the mere scum of the earth.'

Murdoch was sentenced to be executed at the Edinburgh Tolbooth on Wednesday 29th March and then delivered to Dr Munro for dissection. The Lord Justice Clerk said:

'We might have made a lasting example of your body being exposed long in public, but, Sir, it is to be exposed as a public skeleton in the Anatomy Hall, that it may be remembered what an atrocious offender you were.'

According to the reporter, Murdoch seemed little affected with this situation.

The newspaper report concluded:

'The speedy manner in which this daring culprit has been brought to justice, does great honour to the public police of the country.'

The Highest Court in the Land
Source:
Caledonian Mercury, Thursday 4th May 1815 and Thursday 13th July 1815

Until recent years, when the European Court of Justice acquired precedence, the House of Lords was the highest court of appeal in Britain. While it was rare for Linlithgowshire cases to reach this esteemed body it did happen on a number of occasions. After an unsuccessful appeal to the Court of Session, Mr Arbuckle, a timber merchant from Queensferry brought an action in the Lords for:

'wrongous imprisonment, to recover a satisfaction in damages at the common law, or by the statute of 1701, from the defenders, the appellant having been wrongfully charged with having committed a theft, and having been confined in a dungeon appropriated solely for those who had committed the most heinous crimes.'

The Early Years

The trouble had begun in February 1809. Along with a number of other people, Arbuckle was at an auction of wood on Lord Rosebery's estate. He had successfully bid for a number of lots at a total cost of £44 17s 6d. His accusers had also bought a few lots, to a higher value. Arbuckle had left with their four lots instead of his own. The accusers (led by William Taylor, soap boiler) had gone to the local magistrate who had had Arbuckle imprisoned for six days until the matter was cleared up.

Arbuckle was not satisfied simply to have been released, however, believing that he had been badly mistreated. Over the next six years he pursued his complaint through the Scottish courts, seeking damages against Taylor and the other men whose timber he had inadvertently taken, without getting the result he wanted until by 1815 he had arrived at the House of Lords.

In May of that year, the Lords heard Arbuckle's counsel, Sir Samuel Romilly (a great legal reformer and former Solicitor General), argue that the accusation of theft was false, highly injurious and was a result of something which was nothing more than a common mistake, that the prosecution was malicious and that Arbuckle should have been granted bail, as he had requested.

The Solicitor General of Scotland was examined at considerable length. He believed that Taylor had been quite within his rights to bring the charge, his wood having been taken, and this could hardly be considered to be malicious. Regarding bail, he said that it was not clear whether a verbal application had been made but that, in any case, Scots Law made it clear that it could only be granted following a written one, of which there was no record.

There was much discussion over which Acts applied in this case, with reference to other cases. There was debate as to when a bail application could be lodged - did it depend on whether or not the magistrate intended to re-examine the prisoner prior to committing him to a trial? Sir Samuel, possibly feeling he was losing the battle on these points, tried to focus matters on whether it was right that a man should be locked up prior to trial solely on the word of one man without any evidence having been gathered.

The Lord Chancellor postponed judgement and it was not until two months later that the case revived.

By this time some light had been shed on Arbuckle's bail request. It was confirmed that he had indeed made it in writing, as required. He had given it to

The Early Years

a Mr Watson to give to the Sheriff, but unfortunately, Watson had failed to pass it on, meaning that the Sheriff could not be considered to have failed in his duty. All this debate was about procedural matters within the criminal justice system and it was becoming harder and harder to see that Taylor or his co-accusers could be deemed responsible. Despite his determination and perseverance Arbuckle walked away a beaten, and much poorer, man.

Theft in the Early Nineteenth Century (1) – The Oatmeal Thief
Source:
Caledonian Mercury, Monday 10th January 1818

Robert Tenant is introduced to us as a man who had *'previous'* as a former prisoner who had been held in the tolbooth in Linlithgow. Reputation counted for a lot in nineteenth century Scotland, as he was to find to his cost.

Tenant was brought before the High Court of Justiciary in Edinburgh to face the accusation that he had broken into the mill of Binny on the night of Wednesday 19th February 1817 and:

'wickedly and theftuously carrying away 12 bolls or thereby of oatmeal'.

A boll was 140 lbs, or 63.5 kg. 12 bolls was therefore 762 kg – a substantial amount! The goods in question were the property of Archibald Meikle, a farmer from West Binny who leased the mill. Tenant pled not guilty to the charge.

The crime was detected by Archibald Walker, a servant to Archibald Meikle. Walker was in charge of the mill, and had responsibility for locking it up at night. Arriving there on the morning after the theft, he found the door half open. When he went in he found that a considerable quantity of oatmeal (detailed as, 'Six load and ten pecks and a half') had been removed. He examined the door and found that it hadn't been forced, and must have been opened from the inside. He reckoned that the thief must have got in through the roof, and would have to have been someone who knew the building. Walker, of course, made Meikle aware of the incident. He told his master that he suspected Tenant. Why? Because Tenant had been a servant at the mill before him, so would know how to get in. No doubt his criminal record was also an incriminating factor.

Chapter One

Meikle and Walker quickly returned to the scene. Looking outside, rather than inside, the mill, they noticed very clear tracks left by a horse and cart. They set off in pursuit, following them for two miles until they joined the Glasgow road near Uphall. At that point it was impossible to follow them anymore, or even to identify whether the cart had turned east or west when it joined the main road. Meikle sent out his servants to see what they could find and one returned with intelligence that Tenant had been seen heading west with a cart full of meal.

With another servant in tow, Meikle was soon on Tenant's tracks. At Polkemmet toll he heard that Tenant had already passed through, still heading in the same direction. Pressing on, they caught up with him two miles west of Kirk of Shotts.

Now, according to Meikle (supported by his servant), they found Tenant's cart full of meal in Meikle's own sacks. Meikle accused him of stealing the meal and Tenant, making no attempt to deny it, said that it was all there. Meikle and the servant started to unload the sacks and Tenant, far from objecting, helped them. Meikle decided that rather than transport it back to the mill, he would travel on to Airdrie, where he sold it.

Tenant had a different version of events. According to him the meal was his own. He agreed that he had met up with Meikle and Walker on the road but he insisted that he himself, and not Meikle, had gone on to Airdrie and sold the meal. He even remembered that the purchaser had been a man called Dobie.

In any case, Meikle had shortly thereafter made the authorities aware of the crime and Tenant was brought before the Sheriff-substitute of Linlithgowshire for examination, as was common before a trial was set. After this appearance in court, Tenant absconded (which probably didn't help his cause), but was tracked down and brought to trial.

One might have thought that Mr Dobie would have been called as a witness for the defence but for whatever reason this didn't happen. Tenant's lawyer, Mr McNeil, summed up by arguing that there was no evidence that a robbery had even taken place, let alone that Tenant was responsible. However, the jury didn't even feel the need to retire, quickly coming to a guilty verdict. After a suitable exhortation, Tenant was sentenced to transportation for fourteen years for a crime that may not even have been committed.

The Early Years

Theft in the Early Nineteenth Century (2) – Two cases of House Breaking
Source:
Caledonian Mercury, Monday 20th July 1818

On Saturday 16th July Elizabeth Nimmo, described as an interesting young woman of about 20 years of age, was brought to the High Court of Justiciary from Linlithgow jail. She faced accusations that on the 16th of April she had gone into the house of David Gray, a wheelwright and turner in Linlithgow, and stolen a trunk or chest, a white muslin (or blue) gingham gown, a white muslin petticoat, two white dimity bed gowns, and a variety of other articles of wearing apparel, together with a pair of gold ear-rings, and a pocket bible. Quite a haul.

Under examination, she pled guilty to taking all of the goods but said that she hadn't meant to keep them. The Lord Justice Clerk asked her if she meant to say that she had taken them *'in joke'*? Yes, she agreed that was what she meant. The Court was unsure as to whether to take this as a plea of guilty or innocent. In the end it was decided to transfer the case to the Sheriff Court.

That day the High Court also considered the case of Alexander Spence and Peter Liddle, two Linlithgow shoemakers' apprentices. They were accused of housebreaking and theft. Since they had failed to appear they were declared to be outlaws.

Respect for the Law
Source:
Caledonian Mercury, Monday 10th May 1819

Nineteenth century Britain was a very hierarchical society. Crimes against the upper classes, their property or their agents, were taken very seriously. The Caledonian Mercury of Monday 19th May 1819 reports two cases, one from Linlithgowshire and one from Edinburgh, in which lack of respect for men of the law was a significant factor. Two other Edinburgh cases reported in the same article shed interesting light on the judicial values of the day.

On Wednesday 5th May 1819 the Justices of the Peace for Bathgate district fined Robert Millar, a weaver from the town, the substantial sum of £5 plus expenses (to be used for poor relief in the parish).

The Early Years

His crime was to have:

'grossly insulted James Corbet, Esq. one of the Justices of the Peace, in the laudable discharge of his duty as a Magistrate.'

The Justices intended to send him to jail but he displayed such contrition that they let him off with the fine. However, they told the court that they were determined to rigorously execute the law against offenders in future.

The Edinburgh case involved a baker's lad, who was charged with walking on the pavement with a large basket of bread on his head, contrary to police regulations. When challenged by a policeman, he refused to get off the pavement or give his name. The Magistrate declared that:

'nothing can be more dangerous to foot passengers than bakers carrying their bread on large boards and baskets along the foot pavement, and many persons have been injured thereby.'

Really? Nothing? Who would have thought there were so many bread transportation related injuries! To discourage further offences the Magistrate imposed a fine of ten shillings. On the same day, John Duncan, a carter, was fined £1 for allowing his horse, pulling a loaded cart, to wander unattended through the streets of Fountainbridge while he was enjoying a drink at the toll-house. Meanwhile, Robert Symington and James Duff were sentenced to thirty days solitary confinement in Bridewell Prison on bread and water for improperly entering a property in North Richmond Street and stealing a bag of potatoes.

Wanted – Reward Offered
Source:
Caledonian Mercury, Monday 14th June 1819

How serious a problem was theft in the county at this time? We saw in 1802 that it serious enough for there to be a 'Society for Prosecution of Thieves Etc. in the County of Linlithgowshire'. In 1819 it was still fighting the good fight. On Monday 14th of that year, a small ad appeared in the Caledonian Mercury in which the Society offered ten guineas reward for information leading to the arrest and conviction of the perpetrator of a theft in Queensferry. Five nights earlier someone had broken into Mr Alexander Pollock's grocer's shop by a back window and made off with a considerable quantity of goods and some money.

The Early Years

The advert was endorsed by Mr Pollock, who was offering a further five guineas. We may hope for his sake that the villain was apprehended, but if so the national newspapers do not record it.

'Three Desperate Characters'
Source:
Caledonian Mercury, Wednesday 17th June 1819
Aberdeen Journal, Wednesday 28th July 1819
Scotsman, Saturday 24th July 1819 and Saturday 21st August 1819

On Wednesday 17th June the Caledonian Mercury reported the story of James Whiteford, Ralph Woodness and Richard 'Curly' Smith, whom the reporter described as *'three desperate characters'.*

Woodness and Smith were accused of breaking into and robbing a shop in Linlithgow. While being held in Linlithgow jail they met up with Whiteford, who had been arrested on suspicion of an assault and robbery in Hopetoun Wood. The three had formed an alliance and attempted to break out together. They were unsuccessful, but the authorities were somewhat alarmed, and in an effort to prevent them from trying again all three were put in irons. This plan back-fired, however, as the men soon managed to get out of them, and in an ingenious (but undescribed) way converted the irons into instruments for a second attempt! This time they nearly got away, leading the powers that be to conclude that they needed to be transferred to somewhere more secure. They were brought to Edinburgh *'heavily ironed, and under a strong escort.'*

A month later, on 19th July, Woodness and Smith were brought to trial, an event covered by a number of papers. The charge was that on the night of 28th March they had broken into Andrew Edgar's shop and stolen cloth and other goods worth around £350 and with being *'habit and repute thieves'.* Entry had been effected by cutting through a shutter, removing a pane of glass and unbolting the window. The crime was discovered the next morning by the town drummer. At about 5am he was doing his usual rounds when he found a parcel lying in the street near Mr Edgar's shop. He quickly spotted the broken shutter and went to alert the owner. A search of the neighbourhood found that a number of items had been dropped by the thief or thieves in their haste to escape.

At around eight o'clock the next morning Woodness was in Glasgow, arriving by gig at the door of a publican called Sinclair. Sinclair was unavailable so Woodness

The Early Years

spoke to his wife. He brought a number of bundles of goods into the house and asked Mrs Sinclair to look after them for him. Her suspicions were instantly aroused. She sent for her husband and got a number of neighbours to help carry the lot to the local police station. Mr Edgar was able, in the fullness of time, to identify the goods as having come from his shop and a number of witnesses were able to place Woodness and his gig at various points along the route. The jury were unanimous in finding him guilty and he was sentenced to be hung in Linlithgow on Friday 27th August, just over a month after the trial.

The case against Smith was less clear. Some witnesses reported seeing him on the gig with Woodness during the journey but there was no evidence that the two had been together in Linlithgow or Glasgow. As a result the jury returned a verdict of not proven. However, a further charge was hanging over of him of assaulting young girls. The evidence was heard behind closed doors so the journalist was unable to find out, or at least to report, the details. It seems that Smith pleaded guilty and was sentenced to seven years transportation.

What of the third desperate man? Whiteford is described as a stout young man, 24 years of age and from Balerno. He was a married man with two children and a shoemaker by trade. He was accused of breaking and entering, assault and theft. His accusers were Henry Duncan, toll-keeper at the toll-house in Hopetoun Wood, and his sister Mary.

Henry and Mary had been at home, in the toll-house, on the night of 26th to 27th March. At about three in the morning they were woken by Whiteford. He wanted them to give him a bottle of porter, which they did. He then demanded more drink, making a lot of noise, shouting and banging on the window shutter and the door. Not unnaturally, Henry refused to let him in, though he did suggest that Whiteford would probably have more success in a house further down the road. While not exactly neighbourly, it was perhaps a reasonable manoeuvre to try to get an antisocial character to move on.

Whiteford was not to be persuaded and broke one of the shutters, provoking Mary, unwisely, to open the door to remonstrate with him. Whiteford grabbed the chance to push through the half opened door and bludgeoned Mary on the head. He pointed a pistol at Henry and threatened to blow his brains out if he didn't hand over the toll money. Henry opened the chest where the notes were kept and handed over £10 (including a £5 note – something so unusual as to be noteworthy). Not satisfied, Whiteford demanded the coins as well and received a brass box containing £1 in silver and a handful of pennies. Whiteford's final

The Early Years

demands were for bread and whisky, both of which he was given by the terrified Henry.

Whiteford admitted his culpability and could only say in his own defence that the pistol hadn't actually been loaded. Under the circumstances, the jury didn't even feel the need to retire before finding him guilty. Sentencing him to be executed, the Lord Justice Clerk made a most impressive address to the prisoner and warned him to prepare for death, as he could not have the smallest hope for mercy. The sentence was carried out on the 18th August, just before nine in the morning, at Libberton's Wynd in Edinburgh. It is reported that he was fully aware of the enormity of his crime and behaved in a very penitent and resigned manner in the period after his trial.

Chapter Two:
1821-40 – The World Gets Smaller

The World Gets Smaller

Introduction

The twenty years from 1821 to 1840 could be described as Linlithgowshire's Canal Age. The Union Canal was opened in 1822, making transport between Edinburgh and Glasgow faster and cheaper. The canal was only to have a short period of supremacy, however, as just twenty years later the Edinburgh and Glasgow Railway opened. These new transport routes brought the rest of the world closer to the county. In both cases, construction meant a temporary influx of itinerant labourers, many from Ireland and the Highlands, causing tensions between the locals and each other. Linlithgowshire people remained quite capable of committing their own crimes, though, as we will see, incomers to the town were involved in a number of offences – as perpetrators and as victims.

The end of the Napoleonic wars brought a period of peace and stability in Europe, which greatly benefited British merchants and manufacturers. If the early decades of the Industrial Revolution had seen the creation of dark satanic mills where the new industrialists exploited downtrodden workers, the 1820s and 30s saw the tide begin to turn. Trade unions became legal in 1824 and workers' rights began to be established through the passage of Factory Acts.

The first two decades of the century had seen much debate on state of the prisons and their purpose and effectiveness. Thanks to the campaigning of people such as Elizabeth Fry, the Gaols Act was passed in 1823. It was intended to improve conditions and direct the penal system away from punishment and deterrence, towards rehabilitation and reform. However, the lack of an inspection system meant that it had little impact. In any case, the public were not fully convinced by this change of direction. Discussing prisons, Walter Scott wrote in his journal on 20th February 1828:

'I do not...see the propriety of making them dandy places of detention. They should be places of punishment, and that can hardly be if men are lodged better, and fed better than when they are at large.'

The same arguments are made by some people today.

THE WORLD GETS SMALLER

Rape
Source:
Glasgow Herald, Friday19th January 1821

Like today, nineteenth century women were at risk from sexual assault, and gaining a conviction was often problematic. A short account of a case from the High Court of Justiciary in 1821 suggests that a more complex story lay behind the bald facts.

'Andrew Greenfield was placed at the bar, charged with Rape, and with assaulting Sarah Andrews with intent to perpetrating that crime, on the 15th October last, on the high way leading from Linlithgow to Queensferry. The prisoner pled Not Guilty, and the Court, as is usual in such cases, was cleared. We understand that the public prosecutor gave up the case on the examination of the first witness, Sarah Andrews, who declared that the prisoner was not the guilty person.'

Theft in the 1820s
Source:
Caledonian Mercury, Monday 8th August 1825 and Thursday 11th June 1829

Every decade has its sprinkling of cases of theft. Two from the 1820s are detailed below.

The first was a case of agricultural theft heard in the Justice of the Peace Court in Linlithgow on the 2nd August, 1825. On trial was James Wright, a resident of Falkirk and the master of coal boat No. 74, which plied its trade along the Union Canal. He was held in the tolbooth of Linlithgow following an accusation by Mr Robert Jack Lang, Procurator Fiscal, that he had stolen hay. Several witnesses confirmed that they had seen Wright take hay from a field which formed part of Mr John Bartholomew's farm at Greendykes, in Uphall parish; a location conveniently close to the Union Canal. Wright was found guilty and, after a suitable admonition, was sentenced to six weeks imprisonment.

The high majority of the criminals (or at least those convicted of crimes) in this book are men. However, there are a few women and one of them was Helen Dot from Linlithgow. She pled guilty to two acts of theft committed on the 12th and 15th February 1829 in Edinburgh. On the 12th, she had managed to make off with a number of items from a carrier's cart, then on the 15th she had stolen a

The World Gets Smaller

gown from Marion Graham. Though the items taken from the cart are not named this would seem to be fairly low level crime. The judge thought otherwise and sentenced her to seven years transportation. It may have been the fact that she had committed more than one theft that led to such a harsh sentence. In the same paragraph, the paper records the case of George Baird, a gardener, who pled guilty to housebreaking. In the view of the court his crime was:

'aggravated by his being habit and repute a thief, and previously convicted of theft.'

Baird was sentenced to fourteen years transportation.

A Crime Against the Elite - Two Cases of Poaching
Source:
Caledonian Mercury, Monday 26th December 1825 and Saturday 13th December 1828
The Scotsman, Saturday 11th March 1826

While theft of hay from a farmer was one thing, stealing from the local gentry was quite another. On Boxing Day 1825 the Caledonian Mercury reported an exciting incident under the unusually worded heading:

'DESPERATE RENCOUNTER WITH POACHERS'

The incident had taken place only three days earlier, on the Friday before Christmas, between 1 and 2am. The paper describes the men accused as *'three desperate poachers'.* Two of them, John Simpson, a sailor, and William Mason, a nailer, were from Grangepans, while the third, an iron-founder called William Forrester, was from Borrowstouness. They were discovered shooting pheasants in a wood belonging to Major Hamilton Dundas of Duddingstone by three of the gamekeepers of the Earl of Hopetoun. It seems that the Earl was concerned with the threat of poaching, perhaps having experienced losses himself, so had deployed his men at night to catch or scare off potential offenders.

Having heard the poachers' shots, the gamekeepers tracked down and tried to seize them. One gamekeeper grabbed hold of Simpson's gun, no doubt to prevent him turning it on his would be captors. However:

'this daring fellow instantly drew from his pocket a large Spanish folding knife, which it appears he generally carries about with him, and therewith inflicted a severe wound on the keeper's face.'

The World Gets Smaller

Simpson managed to escape but Mason and Forrester were caught and taken to a Justice of the Peace in Linlithgow, along with their bag of freshly shot pheasants. They were questioned and charged, with every likelihood of facing transportation. A warrant was issued for the arrest of Simpson, but as the story went to press he had eluded the vigilance of the constables. Furthermore, the Scotsman article from the following March lists Forrester and Mason among those indicted to stand before the High Court, but no mention is made of Simpson.

It is interesting to note that the possession of guns by poachers did not seem to merit any comment.

Another case of poaching with a number of similarities made the papers in late 1828. This crime was committed on Monday 24th November. Again three people were involved, again they were caught between 1 and 2am, again they were shooting pheasants, and again not all were apprehended. This time the offence took place at Dalmeny Park, part of the Earl of Rosebery's estate. Two of the people managed to evade capture, but William Elder, of Puncheonlaw, in the parish of Kirkliston, was caught by the Earl's gamekeepers.

As in the 1825 case, the gamekeepers decided to take their prisoner to Linlithgow. However, Elder managed to escape by leaping into, and swimming across, the Union Canal. This must have been an unusually deep section as in most parts anyone who is unlucky enough to find him or herself in the canal would be best advised to stand up and climb out. In any case, Elder managed to get away and the authorities were unable to track him down.

After five days on the run Elder decided to give himself up. Perhaps his honesty in coming forward and pleading guilty counted in his favour as he avoided one of the more serious punishments open to the court. For starters, he was sentenced to a term of imprisonment of six weeks in Linlithgow Jail plus a fine of £10, but that wasn't all; in order to be released he had to provide a further £10 as a surety, to be returned to him if he did not reoffend by the end of the following year. £20 was a large sum of money, but if Elder was unable to stump up the fine and the surety he was told he would face another six months in prison. Still, at least it wasn't deportation.

The World Gets Smaller

Multiple Fraud
Source:
The Scotsman, Saturday 6th October 1827
The Examiner (London), Sunday 14th October 1827

Occasionally, a story involving Linlithgowshire even made it into the London press. The Examiner reported the following series of crimes on Sunday 14th October 1827 in its Accidents and Offences column. It had taken the article from a slightly fuller account in the Scotsman.

The villain of the story was a man who went, somewhat ironically, by the name of Walker. He hired a horse in Perth, in the way in which someone might hire a car today. He rode it to Edinburgh where he sold it and pocketed the money: unlike a car, a horse did not have any registration documentation with it, and you didn't need a licence! He then hired another horse and rode to Portobello, where he sold it. Making his way back into town, he hired a third horse, described as a road mare, from Mr Alexander Bullock, a stable owner in Rose Street. He told Bullock that he was heading to Dalkeith, but in fact travelled to Linlithgow. Once again, he sold the mare. The report tells us that he got £4 10s for this sale, which suggests that he had made quite a lot of money by this stage. He had a slight setback here, however, as his Linlithgow purchaser smelt a rat, returned the horse and demanded (and got) his money back.

Walker rode on to Falkirk where he got stabling for the mare at the Cross Keys Inn. With the horse secure in his stable, the landlord then fell for Walker's silver tongue and agreed to lend him £3. With this additional money in his pocket, Walker slipped away on the night mail coach to Glasgow, taking with him a new saddle and bridle that he had managed to get his hands on without paying! The report concludes by saying that Walker has not been since heard of.

From the Scotsman we know a little more: Mr Bullock, you will be glad to know, was reunited with his mare, and we have a description of Walker as aged around 30 to 35, approximately 5 foot 9 inches tall, with a dark complexion and a long face. However, neither paper carried any follow up story so he may have managed to evade detention.

Returning to the Examiner, since we are on a rare trip south of the border, we shall mention the next two stories in the Examiner that day, which deal with two accidents rather than offences.

Firstly, there is the story of Mr Brown, junior, who had taken a balloon flight at Wakefield. Pulling too violently on the valve, he had allowed too much gas to escape and had descended rapidly to earth. Brown had severe injuries to his head and feet.

Secondly, the sad story of Joseph Harwood. A public inquest was held at the Bank public-house, King Street, Bloomsbury into his death three days earlier. Harwood was a forty five year old man:

'of most healthy appearance, a man who often boasted of never having had a day's illness in all his life.'

On the day of his death he had gone for a walk then returned to his seat by the fireside (it is unclear if this was the fireside of his own residence or the Bank). He:

'turned exceedingly pale, complained of a violent pain and sickness of the stomach, and continued in the most excruciating agony for several hours.'

He was put to bed where he passed away soon after. A surgeon was brought in to establish what had brought Harwood to such a sudden and unpleasant end. He concluded that Harwood had suffered from a ruptured blood vessel. The verdict? *'Died by the Visitation of God'.*

Assault and Robbery
Source:
Caledonian Mercury, Saturday 16th July 1831

If everyone agreed on the events in a particular case the life of a judge would be easy and there would be no need for juries. Of course in real life the parties involved usually give very different accounts, and eyewitnesses can give contradictory evidence, making a case difficult to resolve. Traditionally, this is where the Scottish verdict of Not Proven has come in useful as a halfway house between innocent and guilty.

In July 1831 James Brown, a journeyman blacksmith living in Linlithgow, was charged with attacking Peter Love, a dealer in crockeryware, on the road near Easter Whitburn. As well as assault, he was charged with having stolen from him a silver watch, £2 12s in silver and a number of pieces of crockery.

The World Gets Smaller

Love, of course, testified that he had been attacked and robbed, while Brown denied it. A number of witnesses gave evidence that supported the prosecution case, but two gave testimony that supported Brown's not guilty plea. The Crown (prosecuting) counsel declined the opportunity to sum up, saying he left the matter in the hands of the jury. Mr Crawford, Brown's counsel, did address the jury, protesting his client's innocence, then the Lord Justice Clerk summed up. Without needing to leave their box the jury unanimously found the case to be Not Proven. Sadly, the press did not report the details of the case but the Lord Justice Clerk was evidently unimpressed. Addressing the jury he said:

'Gentlemen, the verdict is yours, not mine.'

Incendiarism
Source:
Caledonian Mercury, Monday 2nd January 1832

Some crimes just don't seem to make any sense - there seems no reason why the person should have committed them. A reporter in the Caledonian Mercury on Monday 2nd January 1832 was clearly perplexed by a very rare case of fire raising. The way the case was reported is more revealing than the crime itself. The reporter began by saying:

'INCENDIARISM – We understand that an individual respectably connected was apprehended on Friday and committed to Linlithgow jail, under strong circumstances of suspicion of having set fire to the stackyard of Mr Ross at Borrowstown-mains, near Borrowstowness.'

After his arrest, the unnamed respectably connected individual had been examined by the Sheriff substitute, who decided that the case would come before the Court of Justiciary. The reporter continued:

'It is impossible to assign any reason for the commission of the crime, Mr Ross never having given any cause of offence to the individual apprehended, or any other in his vicinity.'

Seemingly this sort of crime was relatively unknown in Scotland, or amongst Scots people. The reporter informed his readers that:

'This is the second act of incendiarism which has been discovered in Scotland during

the last two years, while many hundreds have taken place in England; and as the first was in Berwickshire, at a small distance from the Border, where English labourers were comparatively numerous, it was very doubtful whether the crime attached to our own countrymen.'

Inconveniently, there was no racial or class excuse on this occasion:

'The person committed to jail for the fire at Borrowstoun-mains, is a native of Scotland, and we are sorry to add that he is above the rank of a labourer, and one whose education should have kept him from such a crime.'

A well connected, well educated, middle class Scotsman committing a motiveless crime? Clearly very hard to believe!

Attempted Highway Robbery
Source:
Caledonian Mercury, Monday 20th October 1834

Not all crime stories get as far as a trial because on some occasions, needless to say, the perpetrator is not apprehended. The Monday 20th October 1834 edition of the Caledonian Mercury brought news of an unsolved crime. Though the headline was *'ATTEMPT AT HIGHWAY ROBBERY',* it could also have been described as an attempt to steal the post, taking us back to the first two cases reported in this book.

The crime had taken place two days earlier, on Saturday night. A post-boy had delivered the mail to Linlithgow and was on his way back to Edinburgh. He was riding one horse and leading a second, showing that the use of a mail coach was not universal. Just outside Winchburgh he saw two men walking down the middle of the road. As he neared them they moved apart, seemingly to let him through. However, as he passed between them one grabbed the bridle of his horse while the other did the same to the one he was leading. The post-boy struck out at his assailant, using his whip to force him to let go. Having freed himself, he spurred his horse and escaped from the scene, leaving the other horse behind.

Before long he met a farm servant driving along on a cart. He persuaded this man to come back with him to the spot where he had been attacked. When they got there they found no sign of the ruffians. Very luckily, they did find the second

The World Gets Smaller

horse, standing beside the road. The robbers seem to have taken out their frustrations on it: the post-boy reported that it looked as if it had been thrown over and rolled in the mud.

Financial Crime
Source:
Caledonian Mercury, Thursday 21st January 1836 and Monday 12th December 1836
The Scotsman, Saturday 3rd December 1836

In the eyes of the law, financial crime was seen as very serious, subject to the most severe punishments short of execution. From 1836 we have two very different cases from Linlithgow. One involved forgery by a poor woman, in the other, one of the leading families of the town was accused of defrauding the tax man. One won, and one lost. Can you guess which?

In January 1836 Ann Watson, or Baillie, from Linlithgow was charged with two acts of uttering forged notes. Chambers Dictionary defines *'utter'*, in this context, as:

'to (try to) pass off (a forged document, etc.) as genuine or put (counterfeit money) into circulation.'

In this case, the crime may have been to forge a promissory note rather than a bank note. In any event, she pled guilty to one charge and the Crown counsel decided to pass the other, knowing that there was nothing further to be gained by proceeding: the court had no discretion in the punishment and Watson was sentenced to transportation for life. That was not necessarily the end of the story, however. Such punishments were subject to review by Crown Officers and, handing down sentence, the magistrate remarked that the prisoner could have *'some hope of mitigation of the punishment from a higher quarter'.* If she was fortunate enough to have her sentence reduced it does not seem to have been recorded in the national newspapers.

The year 1836 closed with a case that involved one of the most important families in Linlithgow. In the dock were none other than Messers Adam and John Dawson, proprietors of St Magdalene's distillery. Adam and John would both become provost of Linlithgow, a role previously held by their father, and then later by Adam's son.

The World Gets Smaller

In 1834 Adam and John's father had transferred the distillery from Bonnytoun Farm to its more familiar position, beside the canal. In 1836 Mr Dawson Senior had died and the reins had been passed over to Adam and John.

The Scotsman covered the story in almost a full page spread – most unusual for a case held in the Justice of the Peace Court - under the headline: *'EXTRAORDINARY EXCISE CASE'*. In fact, the story was deemed so interesting that the Caledonian Mercury repeated it in its entirety (without giving a credit to the originating paper) over a week later.

Whetting the appetite, the article began:

'On Saturday 19th, a case came to be tried before the Justice of the Peace Court of Linlithgow, which is calculated to excite no small interest in the mercantile community.'

The case was brought by Mr Robert Turpie, Supervisor of Excise. He alleged that the Dawsons had increased stock without declaring it – that is to say, they had distilled a quantity of spirits and concealed them from the excise man. Prosecuting was Mr Williamson (Excise Collector), while the Dawsons were represented by J. A. Maconochie, Esquire.

The Dawsons fired the first shot: before the trial could begin they petitioned the court, complaining that they had been charged excise on 110 gallons of spirits that had not been produced, coming to £21 15s 5d. Mr Williamson admitted that this was correct and the court ordered the return of the money. First blood to the Dawsons.

Proceeding to the case in hand, the first witness called was Stephen Youden, an exciseman. Part of Youden's job was to take regular stock surveys in the St Magdalene Distillery. He seems to have done this somewhat more than once a week as his evidence talks about surveys on the 3rd, 10th, 11th and 16th of September. These involved recording the amount of proof spirit and its strength. The key issue was the difference in the amounts found on the last two dates and how that compared to the amounts declared by the Distillery. The prosecuting council asked him to describe his visit on the 11th in some detail.

The day in question had been a Sunday morning, showing that the taxman never rests. Youden had had breakfast at nine o'clock and had gone to the distillery at about ten, where he met his colleague, Mr Campsie. They reckoned that they must have been there for upwards of an hour for, as they told the court, it was hardly possible to take the stock in less time than that. Youden had taken the measures himself, calling them out to Campsie, who wrote them down.

Under lengthy cross-examination by Mr Maconochie, both Youden and Campsie were a bit vague about the details of the survey. Maconochie questioned them in detail about the steps they had gone through that morning and it became clear that neither could remember with any clarity which of them had undertaken each part of the work, or even the order in which they gone round the building, though they maintained that they were confident that they had done it thoroughly. Campsie in particular got annoyed at this line of attack, saying that he didn't see the use of such questions. To him, these were trifling matters which had no bearing on the case.

Maconochie's next line of attack was to ask Campsie if he had taken the mail coach to Edinburgh that morning. Campsie said he could not see the relevance of the question and refused to answer. Maconochie asked again. Campsie said that he did not think he was properly treated in being pressed with such questions. The argument continued:

MACONOCHIE: *I insist that you answer that question, aye or no or tell us why.*

CAMPSIE: *I will not answer that question. I do not think it legal to ask me to do so. I see no use of such quibbles, and I beg leave to decline answering that question.*

MACONOCHIE: *I beg leave again to put that question, and to move that the answer be taken down. Did you go to Edinburgh, and by the mail that morning?*

CAMPSIE: *I decline to answer the question.*

At Maconochie's request the witness was withdrawn while he explained the significance of the question to the court. He wanted to prove that Youden and Campsie had not had time to do the survey properly. Both men admitted that they had not arrived at the distillery before ten, while the mail coach came through Linlithgow at twenty minute to eleven. Given that it was acknowledged that it took a good hour to undertake the survey they simply had not time if Campsie had got on the coach. He said that if Campsie denied being on the coach he (Maconochie) would prove that he (Campsie) had been.

The World Gets Smaller

Campsie was brought back into the witness box and, on being told that he might be imprisoned if he failed to answer, agreed that he had indeed been on the mail coach.

Sheriff Macdonald turned to the witness and said:

'You see, Sir, it was a very pertinent question, since his object was to prove that you could not have taken the survey in the time you were in the distillery.'

Campsie, not helping his cause, replied:

'No, I don't see that. I might have been there at six o'clock in the morning.'

The Sheriff asked the Clerk to check his notes, confirming Campsie had earlier said that it was past ten when he arrived at the distillery. Maconochie continued to cross-examine, forcing Campsie to admit again and again that he could not relate the details of what had been done, in what order and by whom.

This ended the case for the prosecution, who were no doubt feeling that things had not gone as well as they had hoped.

The first witness for the defence was Alex Benny, watchman at the distillery and on duty on the 11th of September. He remembered Youden and Campsie arriving that morning and observed them as they went about their work. His account suggests that they were taking a slap-dash approach. At one point he followed them into the south cellar. Youden was going along the casks calling out the marks upon them, while Campsie followed him with his book in his hand. Neither of them touched the casks (they should have been stirred to ensure an accurate measure of the strength), or even took samples. Each cask had the quantity on it and Campsie merely called *'This will do.'* Benny's most damning evidence concerned the enormous vat No. 1. The vat was so large that it could not be sampled from the south cellar itself; to do so required going up a set of stairs and opening a trap door in the loft. Youden and Campsie had been unable to remember which of them had taken the measure from vat No. 1. According to Benny neither of them could have because to get up the stairs to the trapdoor required going through two doors, both of which were locked and they hadn't asked for the keys.

Benny said that Youden had asked him to keep a look out for the mail coach and let Campsie know when it arrived. This he duly did and saw Campsie head off to

The World Gets Smaller

catch it.

Next on the stand was Robert Meikle, the distillery foreman. He backed up Benny's evidence about vat No. 1, stating that he himself had the two keys in his possession on that day. When asked, he said he reckoned that to do a thorough survey took an hour and a half. The next witness, cellar-man William Campbell went further, saying that to do the job properly took two hours! Campbell, the model of loyalty, said that in his ten years at the distillery he had never seen anything in the behaviour of the Dawsons:

'to lead him to think they acted unfairly towards the revenue'

and that he:

'always considered them perfectly fair, honest, and upright men.'

John Campbell, a clerk to the Dawsons, continued to undermine the accuracy of the work done by the excisemen. According to him, it was well known at the distillery that they generally underestimated the amount of stock – he remembered talking to other people at work about it. He generously conceded that, like anyone else, excisemen could make mistakes. The point of his evidence was to suggest that the amount of stock was higher than recorded in the lead up to the survey of the 16th, and that the difference in amounts was therefore more easily explained.

An excise officer, Alexander Kennedy, was called by the defence. He was stationed at the distillery and agreed that:

'he had never seen anything to induce him to believe that the Messers Dawson had any intention of committing frauds on the revenue.'

At this point prosecuting counsel Williamson rose and addressed the court. He was forced to concede that the survey on the 11th *'had a somewhat bad appearance'.* That said, the figures from the 11th were not very different from those Youden had arrived at on the 10th. Even discounting the survey of the 11th there was still a discrepancy of 32 gallons that could not be accounted for in when they were compared with the results of the survey taken on the 16th.

Maconochie countered that there was no reason to believe the survey results from the 3rd and 10th of September given by a man who had fabricated results on the 11th. The accuracy of the earlier results rested solely on Youden's oath. He suggested that the Dawsons had been the victims of a premeditated plan: a series of progressive underestimates by Youden, the last of which was supported by a colleague, followed by an accurate survey on the 16th designed to incriminate them. He went on to talk about the seriousness of the charges:

'it can never be lost sight of, that a charge of wilful fraud against persons in their situation in life is to the full as severe, if not more so, as a charge of felony against persons of lower rank; and I must say, that it would be without example, as far as I know, that a person should be convicted of a felony upon evidence of a witness whom the prosecutor himself had given up as guilty of wilful and corrupt perjury!'

In the absence of Sheriff Macdonald, W. D. Gillon (Justice of the Peace, and MP) addressed the court to agree that very little trust could be placed on Youden's evidence. Having run over some of the inadequacies in Youden and Campsie's testament he concluded, as reported in the papers:

'It appeared, on the best testimony on which they could rely, the excisemen and men about the distillery, that the character of the defenders was beyond suspicion, and they had never been known to entertain the least desire to defraud the revenue. He might remark also, that, considering the severity of the Excise laws, which were the most harassing possible, it was really too bad that the honest trader should be thus at the mercy of these officers, rendering that which the law made too severe at first, still more harassing and vexatious.'

The Dawsons were cleared of any wrongdoing, though Mr Williamson said, for the record, that the Board of Excise may consider an appeal. No such appeal seems to have been forthcoming, or if it was, it was not reported in the Scotsman, Caledonian Mercury or Glasgow Herald.

A Day in the High Court in 1838
Source:
Caledonian Mercury, Thursday 15th February 1838

An account of one day's proceedings at the High Court of Justiciary shows us the speed at which trials were completed, and, by eliminating differences in date and magistrate, allows comparisons to be made of the sentences for different offences. The day in question is Monday 12th February 1838, where the court rattled through six cases, one of which centred on Linlithgow. The first three were Edinburgh cases.

First up was Margaret Blackhall, habit and repute a thief. For stealing three cast-iron window sash weights from a cellar in the Cowgate she was sentenced to seven years transportation.

Alexander McKay got the same sentence for breaking into John Jeffray's house in Carrubbers Close by means of a false key, and stealing a pair of gloves, a snuff-box and a brooch.

John Spears, another known thief, also got seven years for stealing a pocket bible.

Moving south to Dalkeith, John McDonald, George Smith and Archibald Richmond were convicted of breaking into the shop of gunmaker Thomas Berry, and stealing two powder flasks, eight guns and a pistol. Surely this was a much more serious crime than stealing a bible or some weights? No: seven years transportation.

What would happen to George Allan (habit and repute), facing four charges of housebreaking? The crimes had occurred between June and August the previous year. Charge one: that he had broken into a cellar in Bathgate and stolen 400 pound of sugar. Charge two: that he had stolen 22 yards of cloth from a weaver's shop in Torphichen. Charge three: another cellar break-in, this time in Boarstane, near Linlithgow, from which he had taken a quantity of whisky. Charge four: breaking into a cellar in Linlithgow with intent to steal. This last offence had been his downfall as he had been disturbed at the scene, and though he got away he was arrested soon after. Allan was found guilty on all four counts. As a habitual criminal he was sentenced to fourteen years transportation.

The session was rounded off by the outlawing of Luigi Deschalzo for non-appearance to answer charges of falsehood and forgery. Not a bad day's work!

St Michael is Kinde to Strangers?
– Assault and Robbery in Linlithgow
Source:
Caledonian Mercury, Saturday 17th March 1838

Another Linlithgow crime came before the High Court of Justiciary the following month. On Thursday 15th March 1838 four men stood before the court. Little seems to have been known, or thought worth recording, about the first three men. The paper noted only their names as Charles Stewart, Arthur Corner and John Bruce. The fourth was Alexander McArthur, about whom we are informed that he was, or had lately been, a servant in the household of John Blair, farmer at Kettlestone, Braehead, Linlithgowshire.

Almost six months previously, on the night of the 17th to 18th September 1837, the four of them had fallen into company with Hector Black. Black was a tailor, and a long way from his home in Ardnamurchan. The four men forced, or induced, Black to go on board coal boat No. 25 on the Union Canal, at the Canal Basin. Between there and the Avon Aqueduct they assaulted him and stole from him 26 shillings, a purse, knife, neckcloth, needle-case and thimbles. The prisoners pled not guilty but the evidence presented convinced the jury otherwise. All four were found guilty and the court sentenced them to fourteen years transportation.

The Coming of the Railway
– Tensions, Opportunities and Murder
Source:
Caledonian Mercury, Thursday 14th May 1840 and Saturday 16th May 1840

Two cases in quick succession in 1840 touch on the impact of railway construction in Linlithgow. The first was extremely serious, with a Highland labourer being murdered. The second shows the opportunistic way in which Linlithgow landowners attempted to wring as much money as they could out of the railway company.

We have previously seen cases where guns were used in poaching. A shooting and killing on 23rd February 1840 is one of the earliest firearm related murders in West Lothian[4]. James Dalrymple faced the charge that:

'on the road leading from Linlithgow to Queensferry, near the Burgh Muir toll bar, he did discharge a loaded gun or fowling-piece at Donald Fraser, labourer, whereby he was mortally wounded, and immediately thereafter expired.'

Dalrymple, described as 45 years of age, of a *'decent exterior',* pled not guilty.

The World Gets Smaller

As the Clearances gathered pace many men from the north of Scotland and the islands found themselves labouring in central Scotland on the major projects that were transforming transport and communications across the country. At this time, Linlithgow saw an influx of men from Ireland and the Highlands for the construction of the Edinburgh and Glasgow Railway. The arrival of these men brought tensions between the different communities. The locals feared the labourers were little better than tinkers. The Highlanders and the Irish resented the attitude of the locals and disliked each other. Religious differences also caused flair-ups within and between the groups. This incident demonstrated the uneasy relationship which existed between the Highlanders and the local population.

There was an unusually large number of witnesses in this case and while each had his or her own point of view they can broadly be put into two groups: the Highland labourers and the locals. The differences between them were starkly demonstrated by the fact that some of the Highlanders had to be examined through a translator, Gaelic being their only language. We will tell the story of the events of that evening from both sides, as they described it in court, starting with the Highlanders.

The man who was to lose his life, Donald Fraser, was one of a group of seven railway labourers who were walking along the road into Linlithgow at around six o'clock in the evening. At that time of year sunset is just after half past five so the sky was not fully dark, as confirmed by a number of the witnesses. It would seem that the men were all, or mostly, from the Highlands.

They seem to have had a pleasant afternoon and some of them had had a couple of drinks, though they denied that any of them were drunk. Some of the men were carrying big sticks. At the front of the group were Alexander Fraser and Robert Ross. The trouble started when they were passing a house at Champany and seems, by their accounts, to have come almost from nothing. As they approached, a guard dog started barking, which annoyed them. Robert Ross and Alexander Fraser moved towards the sound of the barking, intending to hit the dog with their sticks, but before they got very far two men emerged from the house, shouting angrily. Though the Highlanders didn't know it, these men were Alexander Dalrymple and his brother James. Alexander Fraser, who did not understand English, found their tone threatening and struck out with his stick, hitting Alexander Dalrymple. The English speakers amongst the labourers reported that man who was struck shouted to the other *'James, James, fetch out the gun'.* Robert Ross was one of those understood the words and urged his companions to get away. As one, the group started running and didn't stop until they had got to Linlithgow. Some of them agreed that as they passed the Burghmuir toll bar something, perhaps a stone or a stick, may have hit its shutters or door, though others heard nothing.

The group stopped, roughly fifteen yards past the toll-house, and talked amongst themselves about what had just happened. For around five minutes there was relative calm then trouble arose from two directions. From the toll house, the men heard the sound of a gun being made ready; from beyond the toll bar, back up the road they had just run down, they heard men's angry voices coming nearer, and the voices of women who were trying to hold them back. Fearing serious trouble, Ross told his companions to make for themselves, meaning that they should scatter and run for it. The angry men moved towards the Highlanders, past the toll bar, then the Highlanders heard a shot ring out and about a foot from Ross, Donald Fraser fell to the ground. Ross tried to help him up but he was already dead. Within seconds, Ross was being beaten by two men with sticks. As he laid Fraser down again the men stepped back, possibly having seen the gravity of the situation. Another man stepped forward, pistol in hand. Ross grabbed him, saying *'You are probably the person who shot this man',* and tried to force him to go with him into Linlithgow. The man threatened to shoot Ross if he didn't let go of him. Ross did let him go, and went back to the body.

At this stage Ross was isolated, his companions having fled. Alexander Fraser had not gone far; he hid in a hedge, but he was spotted by the locals, who attacked him, cutting his head in three places and breaking his arm. Afterward, he was not able to identify his assailants. As things quietened down, some of Ross's group returned and helped him to take Donald Fraser's body into Linlithgow.

The local witnesses put a rather different slant on events. For one thing, they appear to start the story slightly earlier in the evening when a local man called John Wood met two or three men speaking Gaelic about a quarter of a mile from Champany, between six and seven. He was hit by a stick, and some stones were thrown at him as he passed. He soon came upon a second group. The first group shouted back to the second group to catch him, which they did. One of them asked him if he was for fighting. Wood assured them that he was not and they parted with a handshake. Down the road he came upon Sir James Dalyell's gate, fallen to the ground. He had heard a noise which might have been related to this event and strongly suspected that this was the work of the Highlanders. That said, he didn't actually know how long it had been down. However, another witness, a bell maker from Merrilees, also heard a crowd of Gaelic speakers on the

The World Gets Smaller

road and reported that at half past six the gate was still standing, though it was definitely broken down when he passed it eight days later! Since the shooting was generally agreed to have happened at about quarter past six this would seem to suggest that either Mr Wood was confused about events or that he had come across a different group of men. It seems that the defence was making efforts to lay any bad behaviour that they could at the door of Fraser and his friends.

Other witnesses were more reliably tied to the incidents leading to the shooting. A local woman, Jane Flint, was walking along the road, out of Linlithgow towards the Champany. As she approached the accused's (Dalrymple's) house she heard the sounds of many people quarrelling. Wanting to avoid any trouble she went into a neighbouring house, owned by John Hastion and stayed there for about ten minutes while the altercation took place. She heard men shouting and swearing and the noise of sticks or stones. Emerging, she met James Dalrymple and his two brothers, John and William. James told her that *'the vagabonds have near killed my brother'.* He was carrying a gun and seemed to be very angry.

Just after Jane Flint left, John Hastion got another visitor: William Dalrymple's wife, who told him about the assault on her brother-in-law Alexander Dalrymple. He went out and joined the Dalrymple brothers with the aim of arresting the *'Highlandmen'* responsible.

Attention now turned to the toll-house, where the toll-keeper, Thomas Gifford, lived with his family. They testified that this was not the first time that there had been trouble at the toll-house. Stones had been thrown several times and seven weeks before some people had tried to break the door down. Gifford and three of his children, two of his daughters and his nine year old son, John, were asked to describe what they had seen. The court tried to ensure that John understood the seriousness of the situation and gave a truthful account. It is reported that though he was illiterate, presumably implying that he could not meaningfully swear on the bible, he knew that it was a sin to tell lies.

They heard the men run up to the toll-gate and the shutters of the house being hit by sticks or stones, causing them to look out. Thomas went out to remonstrate with the men, armed with a pistol. They struck at him with sticks, which he did his best to dodge. He cocked his pistol to scare the men, but did not fire. This had little effect and the men forced their way past the gate, causing Thomas to retreat. He ran back into the toll-house under a hail of stones. The Highlanders shouted to him that he was *'an old grey headed bastard'* and that

The World Gets Smaller

they were going to *'pull down the house'.* The Giffords sheltered inside while more stones rained down. One, as big as a hat, burst open the bolted door.
More Highlanders arrived, followed by the Dalrymple party. Most of the latter were armed with sticks and James Dalrymple had his pistol. The Gifford girls and other unnamed women tried to pull the Dalrymple party back, fearing that things would get out of hand, but to no avail. Battle was joined and Alexander Dalrymple was seen hitting a man in a hedge. Through the burst door, John Gifford could see James Dalrymple no more than two yards from him. He saw him raise his gun. John Dalrymple cried out *'Take that from Jamie or there will be murder committed!'* Before anyone could move James had fired, hitting a man only about three or four yards in front of him. As John Gifford gave his evidence he broke down in tears at this point. He remembered that when the gun went off he fell to the ground in fear, and found himself facing the dying Donald Fraser. Hastion reported seeing James Dalrymple raise the gun to shoulder height and fire, apparently without taking aim. Even though he was only two yards from James at the time it happened so quickly that he had no chance to stop him.

Police Officer James Nichol was brought to the scene later that night. Arriving at the Dalrymple house at between two and three in the morning he found James still up, though John and Alexander were in bed. He found a gun and examined it, finding that it had been recently fired due to the dampness of the muzzle and the smell of gunpowder. He arrested James, John and Alexander, declaring *'that this is the instrument which has done the deed'.* He also went to Gifford's house where he found a pistol. However, he was satisfied that it had not been used that night.

Back in Linlithgow, Dr Baird was carrying out a post mortem examination on Donald Fraser. He found that the shot had been fired at short range and that the victim had been facing his attacker. The entry point was on the left hand side of his neck. Having extracted 35 pieces of shot, he found it to be a good match with ammunition found at the Dalrymple house.

The next morning, the Giffords found four sticks used in the fighting in the road outside their house, two of them bloodied. One was especially heavy and described as a *'guid muckle thick ane'.* The sticks were later claimed by some of the Highlanders.

The Dalrymple brothers declined to give evidence, other than James himself, and that was only through an ill-judged written statement. According to his account he had not gone as far as the Burghmuir toll on the night of the 23rd February.

The World Gets Smaller

When he went out he did not have anything in his hand, and he definitely did not shoot at anyone that night. He stated that the gun shown in evidence was not his, though it did resemble his brother's!

The defence called three local worthies to speak for the character of the defendant. George Napier, Esq., had known the family (including the brothers' very old, but still living, mother) for twenty years. He believed the character of the family to be generally most respectable. James ran the farm while his brothers worked as wrights. He described James as mild and inoffensive. Dr Andrew Thomson, Burnside, had known James for ten to fifteen years and described him as quiet, sober, industrious, mild and inoffensive in his manners, as were the rest of his family. Sir James Dalyell told the court that the accused's family had been on his estate for about 200 years and that he had never heard anything against his character. Again, James was described as mild and inoffensive. He reported that on the night of the 23rd he had had two gates knocked down. Railway workers were generally troublesome but that night had seen the greatest damage he could recall.

In essence, the defence strategy seems to have been that:

- despite all the witness statements to the contrary, James Dalrymple was not present at the Burghmuir toll bar, he had not been carrying a gun and had not shot anyone
- the Highlanders were a violent, destructive mob, wreaking havoc in their path
- James Dalrymple was a good chap who never said boo to a goose

None of this offered a coherent rebuttal of the earlier evidence.

Witness evidence now being concluded, the prosecuting counsel, Mr Handyside, addressed the jury: that the deceased had died of a gunshot wound was proven, and that James Dalrymple had been present and had fired the shot was sworn to by credible witnesses. The only question he could see was whether or not this was a case of murder or justifiable homicide. Dalrymple's defence that he was not there held no water and in his opinion the jury must come, he was sorry to say, to the same conclusion that he had, that this was a case of murder.

Summing up for the defence, Mr Pat Robertson decided to abandon the stance that James Dalrymple was entirely innocent. Ignoring his client's statement and plea of not guilty, he contended that the jury should return a verdict of culpable homicide. It was for the jury to say:

'with what intention he drew the fatal trigger – they were to look into the heart of the man, and judge whether there was the intention of deliberate murder, or whether the act was not done under excitement, terror or hurry?'

He contrasted the seven lawless Highlanders and their riotous, unprovoked behaviour, with that of James Dalrymple, whose brother had been assaulted and who had set out after them with a view to taking them into custody. He commented on the respectable nature of Dalrymple's character, a man caught up in the confusion and excitement of the moment. He concluded that justice would be done if a verdict of culpable homicide was returned.

One of the three judges, Lord Meadowbank, summed up to the effect that evidence left the jury with little option other than to find Dalrymple guilty of murder. However, he said that they ought to give the prisoner the benefit of any doubts that they might have, and added that they were fully entitled to take his character into account.

It took the jury half an hour to find Dalrymple guilty of murder by a majority of three. However, they unanimously recommended the court to show mercy.

A second judge, Lord Moncrieff, said that this was a most lamentable and piteous case, where a man of good character had behaved inexplicably. However, the prisoner had had time for deliberation, had been warned by his brother and had none-the-less raised a loaded gun to another man and fired it. As the journalist recorded it, Lord Moncrieff felt that:

'if that was not murder then he knew not what it could be called'.

He said that he had no option but to propose that Dalrymple be executed, though the appeal for mercy would be passed on to the advisers of the crown. Lords Medwyn and Meadowbank agreed, the latter adding that he could hold out no great hope for clemency.

It only remained to lay out the details of the execution. The time and place were to be between eight and ten in the morning of Wednesday 3rd June at Linlithgow, with his body to be buried within the jail precincts. Dalrymple, who seemed to have been deeply absorbed in thought during the trial, was taken away.

The World Gets Smaller

It seems clear that all involved regretted the necessity to find Dalrymple guilty of murder. It was probably a matter of relief to many of those involved when, two weeks later, the crown decided to reduce the sentence to transportation for life. After this dark episode, the second case seems almost light hearted.

The construction of the railway did not just create tensions between the townspeople and the labourers, but also, on occasion, between the townspeople and the railway company. One dispute was reported in the Caledonian Mercury when it came to court.

The protagonists were the Edinburgh and Glasgow Railway Company and Mr Thomas Liston, Esq. Mr Liston owned a large house and garden in Linlithgow. The proposed route of the railway ran through his back garden, cutting off about 300 square yards. To complicate matters, within this area Liston had a well, which carried water to a bleaching field at another part of the premises.

Liston and the Company negotiated for sometime over compensation for the land. He offered to accept £105 and the construction of a retaining wall by the railway. The Company agreed to the wall but was only willing to pay £70. With construction work already underway in the area, the Company needed to get the dispute resolved. Both sides continued to stick to their positions and the Company sought to find a solution by applying to the Sheriff for a jury to assess a fair settlement. The action took the form of an assessment of damages. One wonders if the Company were aware that Mr Liston was the Sheriff-Clerk for Linlithgowshire!

The case was heard in Linlithgow Sheriff Court on 8th May and both sides laid out their arguments. Having considered the evidence, the jury came back with a two part judgement. Firstly, they ruled that the Company should pay £95 for the land and construct a wall. On the matter of the well, the Company was given two options, either to secure an equivalent water supply for Mr Liston or to pay him a further £30. In effect, Mr Liston had gone to court looking for £105 and come away with £125! The Company must have regretted taking on a Sheriff-Clerk in his own court.

The State of the (Criminal) Nation
Source:
Caledonian Mercury, Monday 7th May 1838, Saturday 29th May 1838 and Saturday 16th July 1840

We will close this chapter by looking at the broader picture of crime and punishment in Scotland at the end of the period 1821-40 by looking at two articles from the close of the period. Firstly, there was extensive coverage in the Caledonian Mercury on 7th May 1838 of a report by Prisons Commissioner, Mr Hill, on the state of Scotland's prisons. The report took a broad interpretation of its subject and gives a valuable insight into the establishment view of the state of the working classes and their propensity to commit crimes. Secondly, a short summary of the proceedings of one week's work in the Glasgow Circuit Court in 1840 gives an interesting statistical picture.

Mr Hill found that, on the whole, the news was good, though there had been increases in crime in some areas. He attributed this:

'chiefly to the bad state of trade during a greater part of the year, and the strikes among the workmen.'

He noted that in Aberdeen there had been no commercial distress and no strikes and that as a result there had been no increase in crime.

So, was the key factor that some men who had lost their jobs or had their wages cut turned to crime? No! The problem was men banding together in combinations (unions, as we would now call them) and trying to achieve wage levels that were, In his opinion, unsustainable. The solution?

'Much may be done in preventing the evil by employing a few well informed men to give lectures on the subject.'

For Hill, the most odious men were those who:

'look to combinations as a means of living on their fellow-workmen, in the capacity of committeemen etc.'

Or as we would term them, union officials.

At this distance, it may not seem that there was any particular significance to

The World Gets Smaller

the timing of the publication of this report, and the article on it. However, the date is very significant. The following day, on 8th May 1838, the People's Charter was published. This document gave its name to the Chartists, a working-class movement which campaigned for social justice and political equality. There can be little doubt that Mr Hill saw the Chartists and their fellow travellers as the guiding hand behind the combinations and was attempting to link them in the mind of the public with criminality.

Hill's report went on to say that, as a general rule, crime was much less of a problem than in the past. The newspaper informs the reader that:

'his enquiries have almost invariably proved that the offences now committed are of a much milder character than those that were perpetrated thirty or forty years ago; and that the total amount of crime, when compared with the extent of population, has much decreased.'

He found that certain types of offence were more prevalent amongst certain occupations. Carters were more addicted to stealing. Colliers and fishermen frequently committed assaults and other breaches of the peace, generally from drunkenness, though they were for the most part honest. Wandering tinkers:

'have earned so bad a reputation in Scotland that their name is now almost synonymous with thief.'

On the subject of tinkers, the article records that in 1836 a band of nine or ten tinkers had been causing havoc in the Penicuik area, committing many thefts. They had been driven out of the neighbourhood at that time and had made their way to Selkirkshire. Their position there having become untenable they had recently moved on to Linlithgow. This does not seem to have been a success for them as the paragraph concludes by reporting that:

'Some of them have been arrested, and are now in prison.'

The colliers and fishermen do not seem to have been alone in becoming, literally, worse for drink. Indeed, drunkenness, or the desire to get money to become drunk, was seen by Hill as the most direct cause of crime. At the root of most crime, the indirect cause, was:

'ignorance and the want of a cultivated taste for other than mere sensual gratification.'

The former may have something the courts and political leaders could have sought to address. It is unclear what action could have been taken over the latter!

Given the comments in this article about tinkers in Linlithgow in 1838, it is possible that one of their number was George Yorkston, whose case was reported in the Caledonian Mercury on Saturday 29th December that year. Two days earlier he had found himself before the High Court of Justiciary in Edinburgh where he was described as a common thief with a number of previous offences behind him, as he himself admitted to the court. On this occasion, he was charged with breaking into a stable in Linlithgow and stealing a cock and a hen. The break-in element, in combination with his previous history, led the court to lay down a typically harsh sentence of seven years transportation. Not much festive spirit for George.

Finally, the report on the activities of the Glasgow Circuit Court. A short article in the Caledonian Mercury gave figures for 66 cases heard involving 114 people tried in a five day period in 1840. These suggest that either the authorities were exceptionally careful in the cases they brought to court or that the odds were heavily stacked against the defendants.

Sentenced to death	1
Transported for life	3
Transported for 14 years	3
Transported for 10 years	1
Transported for 7 years	57
Imprisonment from 9 to 18 months	26
Outlawed for non-appearance	16
Referred to High Court	1
Not proven or dismissed	6

Chapter Three
1841-60 – Railway Mania and the Birth of the Shale Industry

Railway Mania and the Birth of the Shale Industry

Introduction

The period from 1841 to 1860 was one of economic growth. Though Chartism remained strong in the opening years, and there were some episodes of social unrest, Britain escaped the revolutions that swept across Europe in 1848. This was a period in which more and more parts of the county were linked by railways: the opening of the Edinburgh and Glasgow Railway in 1842 gave easy access to and from these cities and other stops along the line both for people and goods. This was followed by the construction of many more miles of track in the county, including lines to Bathgate and Bo'ness. The 1850s saw the transformation of the south of the county as shale mines opened up, bringing in thousands of people to work and live in new and expanding communities. Sometimes the mix of different groups of incomers and locals proved explosive. Many of the cases in this chapter have links to these social, transport and economic developments. Others reflect the underlying human weaknesses which are evident in every period.

Since the Reformation, the Church of Scotland had dominated the religious field, but that was all to change with the Disruption of 1843, which saw about 40% of the clergy and congregation members leave to form the Free Church. The breaking of this near monopoly gave a greater respectability to nonconformism and a number of other Protestant sects sprang up, or increased their profile and membership. This had important social implications across Scotland because the Church of Scotland had long had a responsibility for social services such as schooling and poor relief. It quickly became clear that it could no longer shoulder this burden in its much weakened form and that the state would need to step in. One result was the creation of the dreaded poor houses as a place of last resort for the poor.

The Scottish penal system was reformed by the 1839 Prisons Act, which brought all the country's jails under the control of a new board. At the centre of the new regime was a new building, the General Prison, which was constructed in Perth in the early 1840s. It was here that all prisoners with long sentences would be held. Over the next forty years the Scottish prison service became increasingly centralised. The 178 prisons in operation in 1839 had reduced in number to 77 by 1860, and to 56 by 1877.

For Linlithgowshire the period was to close with a technological innovation: in 1860 Linlithgow became one of the first towns in Scotland to be lit by gas.

RAILWAY MANIA AND THE BIRTH OF THE SHALE INDUSTRY

Domestic Violence
Source:
Northern Star and Leeds General Advertiser, Saturday 21st May 1842
Caledonian Mercury, Thursday 25th July 1844 and Thursday 14th May 1846

In early Victorian Scotland, as today, and probably at most other times, the greatest threat of violence came from family members. There seems to have been a greater acceptance of domestic violence within society, and it is likely that only a very low proportion was reported. However, when it became so serious as to result in death the authorities could not avoid being involved. Even then, what would be treated as murder today was viewed more leniently at that time. We will start with two fatal assaults in Bathgate in the early 1840s, and a case of persistent abuse leading to death in Uphall in 1845.

Part 1 - Death of a Child – May 1842
The Northern Star and Leeds General Advertiser was a Chartist newspaper which ran from 1837 to 1852. As well as campaigning for increased political rights and improved conditions for the working classes, the newspaper also sought to improve the morality and behaviour of its members, showing that they were as good as the upper classes. The next story is linked to the second set of objectives.

An unnamed man, his wife and a number of witnesses were examined by the authorities in Linlithgow following a tragic death in Bathgate. On the morning of Sunday 8th May the man had been quarrelling with his wife. He was drunk and started assaulting her. She was clinging on to their four month old, who unfortunately caught one of the blows, causing its (no sex reported) death. When the paper went to print the result of the hearing was not known. This did not stop it from denouncing what it clearly saw as the underlying causes of the incident, and the perverse morality of a society which prevented harmless activities while condoning harmful ones:

'How long will our authorities denounce the recreation of a railway train running on Sabbath, and encourage, by their laxity, the selling of ardent spirits on that day, while murder and every other crime, which disgraces human nature, emanates from the practice of open public houses on the Sabbath?'

Part 2 - Culpable Homicide – July 1844
Wednesday 24th July saw Bathgate labourer Dundas McRiner came to court charged with the murder of his wife, Marion Wardrop, on the night of 19th May. The location of the attack was described as being on the stone road which turns

CHAPTER THREE | 69

off from the public road between Bathgate and Linlithgow.

He attacked her:

'with his fists, or with a stick or stone, and inflicted severe blows on her head, face and other parts of her body, and by kicking and trampling upon her, and dashing her head and person against the ground, sides of the road, and against a gate, and dragging or pushing her into a pool of water, and did otherwise maltreat and abuse her, by all which some of her ribs were fractured, and her person so seriously injured, that she soon thereafter died.'

McRiner denied that he had committed murder but pled guilty to the lesser charge of culpable homicide. Unfortunately, the newspaper report does not record his arguments for avoiding the more serious crime – probably he admitted the assault but not the intention to kill. However, the crown counsel accepted his plea and agreed to reduce the charge, a judgement which the magistrates described as exercising prudent and conscientious discretion.

After two witnesses were heard who testified to the quiet and peaceable disposition of the prisoner, and his previous good behaviour, the court had to decide on a sentence. Lord Moncrieff said that this was:

'one of these cases of culpable homicide which stood on the very verge of murder.'

As such, transportation for life would be the normal sentence - after all, this was a serious case involving a prolonged assault against the man's own wife. On the other hand, the previous good character of the prisoner inclined him to be more lenient. Taking the case as a whole, he recommended transportation for 21 years. The Lord Justice Clerk, after addressing the prisoner on the barbarous and savage nature of the attack, and exhorting him to speedy and sincere repentance, concurred with the sentence.

Part 3 - A Wicked Stepmother – May 1846

Catherine McGavin, or Fairley, from Uphall was charged with:

'murder, culpable homicide, and cruel and unnatural treatment of a child of tender years.'

The poor child involved was the daughter of her husband from his previous marriage. Nowadays, we would expect the age of a child to be known to the day but here they were only able to ascertain that she was between two and three years old. From the evidence, a picture emerged of McGavin dishing out abuse over a number of months:

'On many different occasions, in the course of last summer, the prisoner struck the child with brooms and switches, and otherwise mistreated her, by kicking, knocking her against the wall, exposing her to cold, and withholding from her sufficient food – that the poor girl died in consequence.'

The little girl was buried but several days later the authorities, alerted in some way, had her exhumed and a post-mortem was carried out. This found that she had been:

'in an emaciated state' and 'the small intestines almost collapsed'.

The jury found McGavin guilty of culpable homicide, rather than murder, and the court retired to consider sentence. The following week McGavin learned that she had been sentenced to seven years transportation.

This was the same sentence that the court had given to two other prisoners that day. Another Linlithgowshire resident, John Scott, limeburner from Hillhouse, was found guilty of forging a bill of exchange for £50. Despite several character witnesses who spoke very well of him, their lordships felt that a man of his education and intelligence should have known better. The second prisoner was Euphemia Haxton, who had pled guilty to stealing an impressive haul from her lawyer employer: 60 towels, 49 table cloths, 24 pairs of linen sheets, and a great many similar articles. Was either of these crimes really as serious as that committed by McGavin?

A Day in the High Court in 1842
Source:
Caledonian Mercury, Thursday 14th July 1842

We have seen that the judicial system is always kept occupied by a steady stream of thefts. As in the previous chapter, we will compare a number of cases heard on the same day in the same court. The first one involved a local woman.

On Monday 11th July 1842 Margaret Beattie, from Linlithgow, pled guilty to three charges of theft. Taking into account her previous convictions she was sentenced

Railway Mania and the Birth of the Shale Industry

by the High Court of Justiciary to seven years transportation.

That day the court heard three others cases. How would you rank them for seriousness?

- William Sommerville, shoemaker, stole a pair of women's boots – one previous conviction.
- Thomas Flight, nailer, stole two sheep and a cart – no previous convictions.
- Alexander Cummings, flesher, convicted of assisting Thomas Flight – no previous convictions.
- Margaret Anderson and Elizabeth Stewart stole ten shirts and a silk handkerchief – both habit and repute thieves.

The two women were sentenced to seven years transportation, which seems to be pretty standard for the time. Thomas Flight may have considered himself lucky to get away with eighteen months in prison and Alexander Cummings with nine months. The surprisingly lenient sentence was that handed down to William Sommerville – despite his previous conviction he escaped with an eighteen month sentence.

Death in Custody
Source:
Glasgow Herald, Friday 7th March 1845

The cases we have considered so far show that accused prisoners in nineteenth century Scotland did not have a happy outlook. Conviction rates were high and penalties were severe. It should be no surprise that from time to time an accused man decided to end his own life rather than go through the justice system. The Glasgow Herald reported one such case in Linlithgow in 1845.

The story began earlier in the year when a spate of robberies occurred in the town. The perpetrator was not identified with certainty but was widely suspected to be a local young man called Barclay. These suspicions were strengthened by his unexplained disappearance at around the same time. The authorities were therefore keeping a lookout for him and when he reappeared in late February he was taken into custody and held in the town jail.

Over the next few days, he was brought before local magistrates and questioned a number of times about the thefts. They decided that there was sufficient evidence to put him on trial before the High Court of Judiciary. Until the trial he was to be kept in Linlithgow jail.

The sad account of what happened next sheds interesting light on the running of a local jail, and is worth giving verbatim:

'On Monday morning the jailor, as usual, proceeded to his cell to inspect it and ascertain the state of the prisoner; in doing so, he shut the gate to the court, the key of which he put in his pocket, and while he was in the prisoner's cell he allowed him to walk in the lobby. After being satisfied as to the comfort and security of the prisoner, he went to the next cell, when Barclay suddenly closed the door upon him, and fastened it on the outside by a bolt, so that the jailor was imprisoned in the small space; however, as the window communicated with the street, by his cries a number of people were soon collected, but as the outer door of the jail was locked, no-one could gain admission to relieve him. Meantime, Barclay knowing that it would occupy some time to force an entrance, very deliberately prepared means for putting a period to his existence. He first tore his sheets into strips, and having a piece of rope which he had secreted about his person, which showed his pre-determination for self-destruction, he formed a noose, and throwing it over an iron stancheon, he fastened it about his neck, when, mounting on a bucket, he kicked it from under him, and in a few minutes ceased to exist.

The crowd outside meanwhile were endeavouring with powerful instruments to break open the door, and the cool and resolute manner in which Barclay showed his determination to commit suicide gave energy to their exertions, in order to save the infatuated individual; but notwithstanding all their endeavours, he had completed the rash act before the outer door of the jail was forced open, and the jailor relieved from durance.'

This account also illustrates the early Victorian approach to punctuation and sentence length!

Two years later another prisoner was to manage to break out of Linlithgow prison. On Monday 2nd August 1847 the Glasgow Herald reported that James McNeill, who had been serving a sentence in the prison since March, had escaped, taking with him:

'several items of wearing apparel, the property of the Prison Board'.

Would they expect him to leave his prison uniform behind? Apprehended and brought before the High Court of Justiciary, he had an additional four months added to his sentence.

Injury in the Workplace, or Taking on the Dawsons (part 3)
Source:
Caledonian Mercury, Thursday 10th August 1848

In 1808 we saw Adam Dawson senior successfully prosecute a group of carriers who were stealing grain from him. In 1836 we saw the Excise men failing to gain a conviction against his sons John and Adam junior. In 1848 John and Adam were back in court. This time they were accused of negligence leading to the grievous injury of one of their employees, William Nicol.

The injury occurred on 23rd August 1845. At that time Nicol had been employed by the Dawsons for three years as a malt miller in the malt mill which formed part of the St Magdalene's distillery. In order to explain what transpired, Mr Pattinson, the prosecuting counsel, produced a model of the malt mill for the benefit of the court. The key element was a shaft, about 20 inches (51cm) long and 2 ¼ inches (5.7cm) wide. This rotated to drive the crushing rollers. It was held in place by a large wooden washer, 6 ½ inches (16.5cm) across.

On the day in question, Nicol was oiling the rollers when his hand was caught by the washer, and carried round for some minutes, along with the spindle, at a terrifying speed of 150 revolutions per minute. As a result of this horrific accident he lost a significant part of three fingers from his right hand, as well as damaging one finger on his left hand and receiving a number of other injuries. His counsel reported that the accident left him so incapacitated that he was unable to earn a living. He believed that the cause of the incident lay in the construction and maintenance of the machinery. He acknowledged that it was understood by all parties that the job entailed an element of risk, but he contended that the washer should have been boxed off (presumably preventing contact between an employee and the equipment), that it was not adequately maintained, and that for many years it had not been properly attached, leading to the situation where it was possible for it to trap a man's hand.

He contended that Nicol's employers, the Dawsons, had a duty to use all necessary precautions to secure those employed by them from harm. He cited law and legal precedent (Macaulay v. Buist & Co.) and brought witnesses to support the extent of his client's injuries and the defective and dangerous state of the machinery. Finally, he said that Nicol believed that if he had brought the state of the machinery to his employer's attention he would have been *'turned off'* (sacked).

Mr Maitland now began the case for the defence. With the thoroughness one would expect from a lawyer for the Dawsons, he challenged every aspect of the prosecution's arguments. Firstly, he refused to accept that the injuries were as serious as Nicol and Pattinson maintained. To this end, he took evidence from Dr Baird, who had looked after Nicol after the accident and during his recovery. He also showed that once Nicol had recovered he had been given a job at the mill on the same wages (he gave this job up immediately prior to bringing the case) and that Nicol had been quite able to continue his side business as a publican, which he had run for many years. Furthermore, the Dawsons had been generous enough to provide a number of sums of money to Nicol while he was incapacitated.

Secondly, the legislation on the boxing of machinery only applied to factories where children were employed. The employer and the employee knew that there were elements of risk in the work – this was taken into account in the wages.

Thirdly, he took issue with the suggestion that this was a dangerous mill and that the Dawsons had been negligent. In the twenty three years of its operation, this was the first serious accident, making it safer than most mills of its type. A number of the Dawsons' employees were brought in to give testimony in support of this argument.

Fourthly, he stated that it was part of Nicol's job to ensure that the machinery was in good order: if the washer had been loose for sometime he should have ensured that the problem was addressed. Indeed, the Dawsons employed a wright (joiner) at the distillery to undertake any such work that was required - a man whose time Nicol was able to call on. At no time had he complained that the mill was unsafe and, in Maitland's opinion, the suggestion that he would be turned off was simply untrue.

Why had the accident happened? According to Maitland, Nicol often wore large and loose clothing to work and this had led to him getting caught up in the machinery. 'If there was any negligence it was Nicol's and not his employers'.

Railway Mania and the Birth of the Shale Industry

It did not take the jury long to find in favour of the defendants.

Poaching in the 1840s and 50s
Source:
Caledonian Mercury, Monday 2nd April 1849 and Friday 22nd October 1858

In the previous chapter we saw two cases from the mid to late 1820s where poaching was taken very seriously, with transportation a real possibility for offenders, and one man imprisoned for six weeks and fined £10. Here, we will look at the cases heard at the Justice of the Peace Court in Linlithgow in two separate articles – one printed in 1849 and the other in 1858. These show that the crime of poaching remained very much alive through these decades, but the punishments were less severe.

The first 1849 account includes two cases which were heard on the 27th March and a third from two days later.

Three Uphall men, Robert Brownlee, mason, James Mossman junior, wright, and James Lind, shoemaker, were convicted of trespass in pursuit of game upon the farm at Pouflats. This farm lay within the grounds of the Earl of Buchan, in Uphall Parish. They were fined £1 each, and 5s 4d for expenses (totalling 25s 4d).

James Hughes of Winchburgh was caught trespassing on the Earl of Hopetoun's property at Niddry Mains farm. He was fined only 10s, but had to pay expenses of 14s and 6d. The total of 24s 6d makes this punishment almost the same as that of the Uphall men.

On the 29th March, two Bo'ness men, Alexander Jack, pitheadman, and Henry Marshall, baker, were convicted of trespass in pursuit of game on the Kinneil Estate, which belonged to his Grace the Duke of Hamilton. They got off with 10s fines and 7s 6d (totalling 17s 6d) in expenses.

Apart from the leniency of the sentences compared with twenty years previously, two interesting points emerge from these cases. Firstly, where the information is provided, all were men in respectable trades or occupations. Secondly, the nobility were still very major landowners in the area.

Moving on to 1858, Sir William Baillie, Baronet, of Polkemmet, and Alexander Seton, Esq., of Preston, had a busy day judging cases where men were accused of trespassing and being in pursuit of game.

Robert Aitken, Barbauchlaw Row, Thomas Ramage, Woodhead Row, William Gillespie and John Bellany, Northridge, all miners, were found guilty and each fined £2 each and 6s 6d in costs (totalling 46s 6d) for activities on Newhouse Farm.

James Murdoch and James Black, both miners from Northridge were accused of the same crime on the farm of Cowdenhead. Murdoch was fined 21s with costs of 19s (a total of 40s). Black, most unusually, was acquitted.

James Pringle, an engine-keeper from Whitham was found guilty of this offence on Torbanehill Mains farm and fined 32s plus 14s 6d of costs (a total of 46s 6d).

William Carmichael, a miner from Armadale, had been poaching on Newhouse and Over Hillhouse Farms. His punishment was a fine of 26s and 14s costs (40s, in total).

Finally, Peter Fenwick, a miner from Whitham[5], was found guilty of trespassing on Springfield, a farm owned by the court's magistrate Sir William Baillie which formed part of his Polkemmet estate. He was fined a whopping £2 and costs.

Comparing these cases with those from 1849 there are two major differences. Firstly, the later punishments were more severe, around £1, or 80% higher. Secondly, the poachers were lower in class, at least on this occasion, and as miners there is a good chance that they were incomers, quite possibly from Ireland or the Highlands. Sadly, their social status and origins may have been partially responsible for the harsher punishment.

Alcohol, Public Houses and Public Order
Source:
Caledonian Mercury, Monday 2nd April 1849, Thursday 29th January 1852 (from the Glasgow Herald), Friday 12th April 1850 and Thursday 5th March 1857
Glasgow Herald, Wednesday 22nd August 1860

Alcohol played a major part in Scottish life in the nineteenth century, and was far less regulated than it is today. There were limits, however, and when the authorities believed that things were getting out of hand they stepped in. On 2nd April 1849 the Caledonian Mercury reported two cases which had come

Railway Mania and the Birth of the Shale Industry

before the Justice of the Peace Court. On 27th March publican John Thomson, from Blackburn, was fined 25s, with 12s 6d of expenses for:

'entertaining people in his house at unseasonable hours'.

In other words, keeping his pub open late into the night.

Two days later, Bo'ness publican Henry Peddie was convicted of the same offence and given the same fine but with lower expenses of 9s 6d. These were by no means isolated incidents. It would seem that 25s remained the fine for this crime for some time. Eight years later, Tuesday 3rd March 1857, Linlithgow Justice of the Peace Court heard three cases of publicans failing to close at 11pm. William Wallace of Bo'ness, John Anderson of Bathgate and Janet Bryson, or Rankine, of Bathgate were all fined the standard amount, with costs.

As well as opening too late, there were also occasions when trouble boiled over and the officers of the law needed to intervene. One such case occurred, with tragic consequences, in January 1852. On Tuesday night/Wednesday morning of the 20th to 21st, Mr Carr, a sergeant in the Linlithgow rural police force, had cleared out a disorderly house in Bathgate. Later that evening, he was attacked from behind by four Irish colliers who had been socialising in the establishment. His skull was cracked and, as the paper went to press, he was dangerously ill. The four scoundrels (as the newspaper described them) had fled the town. The newspaper reported that:

'Carr was an active and vigilant officer, and for this reason was obnoxious to the disreputable characters of the village.'

The third story in this group involves the production rather than the consumption of alcohol. We last saw the gentlemen of the Inland Revenue fighting a losing battle against local business magnates, the Dawsons. A case from 1850, reported first in the Scotsman and then the Glasgow Herald, saw them take on an easier target.

According to the newspaper reports, rumours had been circulating about the illicit distillation of whisky in the Bathgate area. Following up on local intelligence, on 1st April 1850 the Linlithgowshire Inland Revenue Supervisor, Mr Alexander Fraser, accompanied by a number of his Bathgate based officers, made a raid on a house occupied by a man named Cuddie or Cuthbert. There they found:

'a 30 gallon tin still, with head and excellent copper worm, a mash tun, two fermenting tuns, a quantity of bruised oats, and some fresh yeast, and feints.'

Though they did not find any whisky, they deduced, from the supplies, that Cuddie was about to start up another batch. They seized the equipment, but were unable to do the same to Mr Cuddie, who had slipped away unobserved. For the journalist, what was most shocking about this affair was that Cuddie had been producing his moonshine:

'within a few hundred yards of the residence of one of our most active county magistrates'.

The following day, Fraser and his men carried out another raid, finding a small still:

'artfully concealed in the workshop and dwelling house of a blacksmith near Bridgehouse Castle, four miles from Bathgate.'

Lest we fear for the moral health of West Lothian, the reporter hastens to reassure us that:

'Illicit distillation is of rare occurrence in this county.'

Of course, the authorities had to remain vigilant. A case from the end of the period covered by this chapter shows that an exciseman's work is never done. Graham Stewart of Torphichen was fined a massive £25 for selling spirits without a license within his house.

Murder on the Canal
Source:
The Scotsman, Saturday 5th May 1849
Preston Guardian, Saturday 19th May 1849

In May 1849, the Scotsman and the Preston Guardian were able to report the solution to a murder mystery which had defeated the police for over eighteen months when a witness came forward with fresh evidence.

The naked body of Euphemia Bourhill, aged between forty and fifty, had been found in the Union Canal at Causewayhead, near Falkirk, in mid October 1847, with wounds on her head and face and a deep gash in her throat. Enquiries at the time had been unable to get to the bottom of this apparent murder. All that could be established was that Bourhill, a gingerbread seller from Edinburgh, had been plying her trade at the Mid Calder fair and had last been seen alive making her way home, near Hermiston. How she died and how her body came to be found in the Falkirk area remained a mystery.

Hopes were raised for a resolution in May 1849 when a lad, reportedly about eighteen years of age, came forward. He worked on the Union Canal, driving horses which pulled the barges. In his deposition he stated that on the evening of the murder he had been at Hermiston, leading the horses pulling a barge crewed by James Gray, Mungo Duff and James Turnbull. He had seen the victim board the boat, even though it was heading west and she was looking for a lift in the opposite direction. The lad was unable to see how events unfolded, due to the distance between the horses and the barge. However, when night fell he went on board and found the body of the wretched woman lying, mutilated, in the boat, with blood coming out of the wounds. She seemed to be quite dead. The crew threatened him with the same fate if he told anyone, and as a reward for keeping quiet they offered him the miserable bribe of one shilling (of the sixteen that they told him they had stolen from her). He recounted that the murderers tore off her clothes to help clean up the blood and then threw her body overboard, into the canal.

Why had the lad come forward at this time? Two factors may have played a part. The papers suggest that he may have been motivated by never having been paid his shilling! However, a second factor might possibly have been that Gray had recently been imprisoned for theft. If he was the ring leader then the lad may have felt that it was now safe to come forward. Turnbull was arrested in Linlithgow and Duff at Ratho. How did the case conclude? Sadly the newspapers are silent on the matter.

The Dangers of Rail Travel
Source:
Caledonian Mercury, Monday 1st April 1850, Monday 15th April 1850 and Monday 3rd August 1854

Three stories from this period illustrate the types of bad behaviour that could occur on the railways, to the discomfort of staff and other passengers. The first two are in effect the beginning and end of the same story. They involve the same party getting involved in incidents in Linlithgow, Edinburgh and on the journey between the two stations, which resulted in two trials. The third is entirely separate, but sheds an interesting light on rail travel at this time.

The cases within this book which received the greatest newspaper coverage tended to be those involving the most serious crimes, such as murder, and which were heard in the High Court. The events of the evening of 29th November into the morning of 30th November 1849 did not reach such heights, and resulted in two hearings in the Sheriff Courts of Edinburgh and Linlithgow, yet they received more column inches than almost any crime related to Linlithgowshire in the nineteenth century. The reason? Celebrities, or, at least, members of the upper classes, disgracing themselves publicly. Two jurisdictions were involved because the incident began in Linlithgow and finished at Waverley Station in Edinburgh. The case for the later action was heard first, but in the interest of telling the events in order we will begin with the Linlithgow case, heard two weeks after.

The Upper Classes At Play
– Part 1: Disorder in Linlithgow

On Thursday 11th April 1850 Sir William H. Don, Baronet, appeared before Sheriff Cay and a jury at Linlithgow Sheriff Court. He was accused of malicious mischief and also wanton and reckless mischief, and finally of a breach of the peace. Sir William pled not guilty, a jury was empanelled, the trial began, and the events of the night were recounted.

On the evening of 29th November 1849, a group of upper class men had been dining in the Star and Garter. The dinner was held by the Linlithgow and Stirlingshire Hunt, which used the hotel as a regular meeting place. The minute books of the Edinburgh and Glasgow Railway Company show that Linlithgow Station was no stranger to incidents caused by the boisterous upper class at play, as they returned home from these, and similar, nights out. Previous events may have convinced them that they had little to fear from the authorities but on this occasion they went too far.

Sir William Don was one of the party and, as the meal broke up, he and a number of other gentlemen made the short journey up to the station to return to Edinburgh on the ten o'clock train (that is, the train which had left Glasgow at 10pm). It was at this point that the trouble began. A great many witnesses were heard in court and they can be divided into the party of gentlemen and those unfortunate enough to encounter them. Though the basic facts were agreed upon there was considerable disagreement about many of the details, and in particular over the tone of the proceedings. Also, some of the gentlemen disagreed with each other on key points, perhaps due to the attention they had paid to the wine list at the hotel. To be fair to the gentlemen, some of their accounts were very similar to those of the railway staff and fellow passengers.

On the night in question, Mr Young, the station master, was in his room, behind the counter of the ticket office, which unlike today was on the upper floor, at platform level. He was going through his paperwork, waiting for the Edinburgh train to arrive from Glasgow when, at about 10 or 20 past 11pm, he heard people moving on the stair below. He heard a pane of glass being broken after which two or three men came into the ticket office. He identified one as the accused. When Sir William walked past the ticket counter with an indifferent air, Mr Young asked him if he required a ticket, to which Sir William replied that he had a return. Mr Young sent one of the porters, Hugh Masterton, down stairs to see what had broken. He quickly returned and reported that the damage was to two panes in each of the lower windows. Mr Young thought it very likely that Sir William was the culprit though didn't directly accuse him:

'but looked him pretty broadly in the face as much as to say he was the party who had done it.'

At this point, they were joined by a number of other gentlemen, bringing the total up to about ten. Mr Young was able to recognise a number of them: Mr Ramsay of Barton (who had passed away in the period between the night in question and the trial), Sir John Dick Lauder, Professor Lizars, Captain Stirling Stewart and Lord Gilbert Kennedy, to whom we can add from other accounts Sir Alexander Gibson Maitland of Cliftonhall and Mr Morritt – an impressive bunch for Linlithgow Station!

It being a cold evening, Mr Young had a stove burning. Sir William took down a notice board from the wall and placed it over the stove, causing Mr Young to fear that it would catch fire. Meanwhile, he was trying to serve a number of the gentlemen who were asking for tickets. Captain Stewart jumped over the counter, putting out a gas lamp, and started messing about with the telegraph wires. Mr Young begged him to stop as they were fragile and pulling could easily bring down the apparatus. The Captain threatened to hit him over the head with his cane, though he didn't actually do so, but instead picked up a ruler and rattled his hat with it. As this was happening, Sir William had opened the door to the back office and had come through, putting out another gas light and making the room rather dark. Some of the other gentlemen seem to have thought that this was a great lark as they started going round putting out the other lamps, while Mr Young and his porters ran round relighting them. As this chaotic dance continued some of the lights were put out and relit two or three times! With the low levels of light and the smoke of the gentlemen's cigars it was hard to see who the main culprits were. To add to the sensory confusion, many of the men were singing in what they considered to be a hearty way. Meanwhile, Sir William had started playing with the telegraph equipment, ringing the bell and turning the handles. One of the gentlemen asked him to stop, remarking that there was no fun in that.

Mr Young was stopped by Lord Gilbert Kennedy, who wanted a ticket. Mr Young asked him to have patience until all the lights were relit. Lord Kennedy was not inclined to wait and hit Mr Young over the head with his cane. Rather daringly, Mr Young grabbed the cane from him and returned the compliment!

By now, the floor of the back office was strewn with notices that had been taken from the walls, presumably by Sir William and Captain Stewart. Masterton, the porter, tried to persuade Sir William to leave the office, but to no avail. With a piece of quick thinking, Masterton went to the platform and rang the bell, as if the train was coming. When the party had jostled their way outside Masterton slipped back in, shut the door and put it on the snib. The gentlemen soon realised that they had been tricked so they started shouting, kicking the door and ringing the bell. The key to the door was in the lock on the platform side, but wouldn't open the door while the snib was on. When the men found that the key wouldn't work one of them took it from the door and threw it as hard as he could. It was found the next day in a garden on the opposite side of the track. Mr Ramsay took the bell which had been used to trick them, and after dancing round the platform with it he put it in his pocket.

The gentlemen weren't the only passengers waiting for the train at the time. Asked to describe the mood of the party, one witness said that he felt that they were in high spirits rather than violent. He described them as:

'just hearty coming from dinner or supper'.

Still, he also admitted that he felt afraid to interfere.

After ten minutes the train arrived. The compartments only held six people but seven of the gentlemen went into one carriage and three into another. The seven were Sir William, the late Mr Ramsay, Professor Lizars, Sir Alexander Gibson

Railway Mania and the Birth of the Shale Industry

Maitland, Mr Moritt, Sir John Dick Lauder and Captain Stewart. Mr Young noticed that the bell had been taken. Rather bravely, he approached the overloaded compartment and asked for it back. All he got for his trouble was, as he described it, *'an extraordinary volley of oaths'*. He then asked them to at least ring it themselves, as the train would not otherwise start! This did not have a positive effect either, and the train did in fact manage to depart. With the station quiet again, Mr Young had a chance to investigate the damage. He was most surprised to find fragments of boiled potatoes on the stairs with the broken panes of glass. This mystery was quickly solved by the testimony of John McDougal, an underwaiter at the Star and Garter. He remembered the gentlemen dining there that night and:

'When the party left he observed Sir William take some boiled potatoes away with him in his pocket.'!

After the high jinks at the station the men kept the party going on the train. Not having a seat, Captain Stewart lay along the legs of some of the others. Shortly afterwards the vandalism of the carriage began. It seems to have been admitted by pretty much all of them that the only one of the seven who was innocent was Professor Lizars, who slept through the whole thing.

As the train reached Winchburgh, Mr Ramsay gave Sir William the bell, which he then threw out of the window: it was found lying near the track the next day. The hat-straps were pulled off and followed the bell out onto the line, as did the curtains. In what would seem like a remarkable feat of dexterity, it was reported that Captain Stewart had unintentionally kicked out the lamp on the roof. Sir William climbed out through the window and up onto the roof of the moving train to put it back, before climbing back in. Joining in the fun, Sir John Dick Lauder pushed the rug out of the window and somewhere around Ratho, as they ran short of material, someone threw Sir John's hat out.

William Jesse Bassett was the unfortunate guard that night. He saw the ten men join the train in Linlithgow and did not notice anything out of the ordinary about their behaviour. He was quite sure that the centre carriage, the one which seven men had entered, was in good condition before Linlithgow. However, when he checked it at Edinburgh, after the party had left, he found that the window-curtains and brass-rods, the straps, and the rugs were missing, and that the lamp-globe was cracked. Much more was heard from Mr Bassett in the second hearing, which we will return to later.

Sir William himself had been questioned by the authorities on 22nd January, at which time:

'he declined respectfully to answer any questions put to him, as he understood the object was to obtain from him a declaration which might be afterwards used against him, protesting, at the same time, that no unfavourable inference was to be deduced from his silence.'

As he was still unwilling to answer questions this closed the case for the prosecution.

Counsel for the Crown, Mr Cleghorn, summed up saying that he felt he had an extremely disagreeable duty to discharge. With some delicacy he went on to say that:

'an investigation into the circumstances that took place on the night of the 29th November was not one that could be agreeable to any of the parties concerned.'

On the three charges, he felt that malicious mischief had been clearly demonstrated by the evidence – he advised the jury that this charge often applied to cases where property was wilfully and deliberately destroyed, even though there might be no malice towards the owner of the property. He then showed how the different pieces of evidence related to the other charges, of wanton and reckless mischief, and a breach of the peace. He admitted that it was not possible to trace every individual act to Sir William but painted him as the moving force behind them and as *'apparently the widest awake'*, by which he would seem to mean the least drunk.

Sir William's counsel, Mr Neaves spoke in reply. He reminded the jury that they were sitting in a court of law and of the seriousness of their decision. He told them that they were not there to judge whether the conduct of the party, of whom his client had been singled out, was correct and irreproachable, or improper and imprudent. In fact he was sure that if the gentlemen involved would take his advice, or that of the jury, they:

'would be advised that the sooner they discontinued these youthful frolics the better.'

No, they were in the court to decide if the public prosecutor had proven the criminal case against Sir William. He described *'malicious mischief'* as:

'the crime of men who, having an ill-will towards their masters, burned their mills, or killed and strangled their cattle.'

By his definition it was really only a crime that lower class people could commit against their betters! He contended that without deliberate malice there could not be malicious mischief and that in this case no evidence of malice had been presented. He described the affair as a good-humoured frolic in which no-one was hurt. He argued that there was as much malicious mischief in the action of the ingenious porter who rang the bell, tricking the men out onto the platform and then locked the door behind them. Surely it was natural that on a cold night the men would not be best pleased and would try to get back inside? He then:

'humorously criticised the evidence in detail, and contended that the circumstances were altogether so puerile as to make such charges as those contained in the libel ridiculous.'

He pointed out that more serious and substantive charges, such as molesting the railway officers in the discharge of their duty, had not been brought because, in his view, the evidence was too weak. He entreated the jury to do justice by his client, treating him neither more nor less favourably because of his social position.

Finally, it was the turn of the Sheriff to sum up. He started by instructing the jurors to disregard any accounts that *'they might have heard out of doors regarding this matter'* as he knew that wild and exaggerated reports had been circulating. He then made some interesting remarks about the importance of the charges. The journalist wrote:

'He wished especially to remark that although the individual acts taken separately might be considered of a light description, all acts that tended to the disturbance of a railway station, and to the obstruction of railway lines, were of such a kind that it was necessary they should be thoroughly investigated, and brought under the review of a court of justice, because they might be attended with serious damage both to persons and property. This was a new mode of travelling, requiring ten times the amount of care and vigilance that was formerly bestowed on means of transit; and it was therefore proper and necessary that those engaged in conducting it should be protected from all improper interference in the discharge of their duties.'

Turning to the charges, he gave the jury instruction in how to understand malicious mischief. He described it as:

'mischief done intentionally, when the act was necessarily productive of injury to property.'

To be guilty, the perpetrator needed to be acting intentionally, to know that what they were doing would cause damage and that they had no lawful right or excuse for their actions. Wanton and reckless mischief, he described as actions somewhat less serious than the first charge, comprising reckless behaviour with a:

'careless indifference to probable or possible consequences.'

Breach of the peace included *'every violation of the public tranquillity',* including riotous conduct or brawling. He commented that the events at the station were:

'attended with great uproar, noise, and disorder, and to the great alarm and disturbance of the railway servants and others.'

He advised the jury that they could find the accused guilty of breach of the peace along with either or both of the other charges. He further instructed them that they did not need to find him to have been a principal actor in the disturbance – if a breach of the peace had occurred and he was one of the offending party then he was guilty. After he had gone through the evidence in detail, he sent the jury out to consider their verdict.

It might seem to the modern reader that this evidence for at least some of the charges was strong and uncontested. However, after a mere fifteen minutes, the jury returned majority verdicts of not proven on all three counts. From a distance of over a century and a half one can't help wondering whether the same verdicts would have been reached had this been a group of railway navvies. It is also debatable whether the judge would have spoken to a less esteemed man in the same way that he did to Sir William, expressing his great relief and satisfaction at the verdict, relieving him, as it did, of the duty to act in a way which would be:

'very painful to himself and what must have been very unpleasant to the party at the bar.'

As a result of the not proven, rather than not guilty, verdict it was required of him to reprove the defendant. We have seen that judges were well experienced in handing down self-righteous admonishments. In the case of a gentleman as fine as Sir William, all the Sheriff could bring himself to say was that he hoped that his conduct:

'might not be such as might again place him in such a position as he had occupied that day.'

The report concludes by recording that Sir William bowed respectfully to the court, and then left the bar, in company with several of his friends who were present.

The trial lasted from ten until five o'clock.

The Upper Classes At Play
– Part 2: Assault at Waverley Station

Two weeks earlier, Sir John Dick Lauder, Bart. of Fountainhall and Grange had appeared in the Sheriff Court in Edinburgh in relation to events which had taken place at the end of this *'good-humoured frolic',* to quote Sir William's defence counsel.

Sir John was charged with wicked and felonious assault against William Jesse Bassett, who you may recall was the guard on the train that night (29th November 1849). According to the charge sheet, Sir John had struck William three times and kicked him in or near the groin or abdomen. Sir John's lawyers had tried to negotiate the charge down to simple, rather than aggravated and injurious assault, but the Crown lawyers had decided to prosecute him on the more serious offence. The counsels the same men who would cross swords in the Linlithgow case reported above: Mr Cleghorn spoke for the prosecution and Mr Neaves, along with Mr Adam Anderson, spoke for the defence. The case had aroused a lot of public interest and the court room was crowded.

As we heard, when the train arrived in Edinburgh it was part of Mr Bassett's duty to examine the carriages, to see that everything was alright. The destruction meted out by Sir John and his companions is described above: fixtures and fittings had been damaged or thrown from the train. While observing this scene of desolation, Mr Bassett met Sir John, who had returned to try and find his hat (in the later case in Linlithgow we would hear that it had in fact been thrown from the train at Ratho). Mr Bassett told him that because of the damage done to the carriage he would need to detain him until he had further orders. Sir John said that he had no right to stop him from going on his way and denied that he was one of the party who had been in the carriage (which perhaps begs the question as to why he thought his hat might be in it!) Bassett described Sir John as being in an excited state of mind, and was unable to say that he was entirely sober.

Railway Mania and the Birth of the Shale Industry

Mr Bassett sent for two policemen but they refused to act, saying that the damage had taken place before the train had entered their jurisdiction of the city of Edinburgh. One wonders how they could tell - this would appear to be a piece of deduction which a lawyer would enjoy examining. It would seem that they may well have simply been reluctant to get involved.

In any case, Mr Bassett's next move was to send word to the railway company agent, Mr Stewart, asking for advice. Sir John did not want to wait and kept trying to leave but Mr Bassett kept moving to block him. Sir John became irritated, grabbed the guard by the collar and shook him several times before one of the policemen was able to place himself between them. Sir John kept trying to get at Mr Bassett, trying to land kicks and punches and Mr Bassett demanded that the police held Sir John for assault, since this had clearly occurred within the city therefore came under their jurisdiction. The policemen agreed that they would take charge of Sir John until the messenger returned from Mr Stewart. The policemen gave a different account from Mr Bassett on the seriousness of the assault, saying that they had not seen any punches or kicks find their mark while he, as per the charge sheet, said he had been punched three times and kicked in the groin or abdomen. His version of events was, however, supported by a porter.

Before long, word came instructing Bassett to take Sir John's card (which, of course, every gentleman carried) and let him go. The swap was made – Bassett got the card and Sir John got his freedom.

How badly injured was Mr Bassett? He reported that after the kick he felt sick for about two hours, and was still in some pain on the Saturday, when he went to call on Sir John at Grange House. He did not make any claim to lasting injury and had not felt the need to consult a doctor (for which, of course, he would have had to pay).

Confronted by his victim, Sir John had said that he was very sorry and that he would make it up to him. At a later date, Mr Bassett was given £5 by Sir John, via Mr Stewart. Bassett declared himself quite satisfied with this compensation he had received.

Meanwhile, back at the station Mr Latham, the secretary and manager of the railway company, had been made aware of the damage to the carriage and the assault on a guard the previous night. He backed Mr Bassett's actions to the hilt. He told the court that if a guard found a carriage to be damaged it was his duty to report it to the station master, whose job it was to decide what action to take.

Railway Mania and the Birth of the Shale Industry

Mr Latham wrote to Sir John, saying that his bad conduct meant that he had the very disagreeable duty of reporting the matter to the board. Two days later he got a reply from Sir John. The letter said that he (Sir John) had called at the station the morning after the assault to try and explain his conduct, but had not been able to find either the station master or the guard. He had been busy for the rest of the day and on the day after the guard had called at his house. He had told the guard that he had done wrong in striking him and promised him compensation. With regard to the carriage, he said, in the letter, that his role had been to limit the damage being done, but that if he was told the cost of repair he would settle it.

Sir John declined to answer questions in court. Instead a declaration which he had written on 6th March was read to the court, for what it was worth. In it he indicated that since the events had occurred so long before he could not give a distinct statement on the subject!

For the prosecution, Mr Cleghorn addressed the jury. He told them that the case involved a serious charge for which no justification had been offered. Mr Bassett had simply been trying to discharge his duties when he had been the victim of an unprovoked attack. Sir John's letter to Mr Latham, along with his agreement to pay compensation, proved his guilt, and even though Mr Bassett had expressed himself satisfied with the money:

'when a party infringed on the values of peaceable society, there was something more required than mere satisfaction to the party receiving the injury.'

For the defence, Mr Anderson took a similar line to that which his colleague Mr Neaves would take a fortnight later in defence of Sir William Don, stating that he sought nothing more than justice, that his client should be judged by the same rule that judged any other man, rich or poor. He argued that Sir John's behaviour was quite justifiable – Sir John maintained his innocence of having damaged the carriage, had offered his card, and if the police did not see fit to get involved then what right did a guard have to detain him? He raised questions over Mr Bassett's evidence and significant differences in the account given by of the police. He said that Sir John had written a very gentlemanly letter to Mr Latham and that this had been rewarded by being used against him!

The Sheriff summed up the evidence. Begging them to ignore any rumours which they had heard about the case, he instructed the jurors to consider nothing more than the evidence before them. He could not go as far as Mr

Railway Mania and the Birth of the Shale Industry

Anderson is saying that Mr Bassett did not have the right to detain Sir John until he had received instructions. He believed that the guard had not exceeded his duties, or that he had offered verbal provocation and he left it to the jury to decide the seriousness of the blows, or pushes, made by Sir John on Mr Bassett. However, there was no doubt that the letter to Mr Latham contained an admission of having struck the guard, although not of having kicked him. He also commented on Sir John's honourably expressed desire to make reparation for any misconduct.

The jury took twenty minutes to find Sir John guilty of assault, but without the kick or the aggravation. In effect, this was what he had tried to plea-bargain for.

The Sheriff spoke of the painful duty he now had to discharge. He hoped that he could pass sentence impartially, but he had known Sir John since he was an infant, which:

'rendered the task imposed upon him a very bitter one.'

He could not help remarking that in some aspects the case was a bad one. Continuing that:

'It was a case in which a gentleman in a high position in society, of education and of excellent parts, had forgotten the temper and dignity which became that position, and had lifted his hand in violence against one who should rather have been taught by him courtesy and magnanimity which should prevail among all.'

However, it was not so aggravated as many which were tried every day in the Police Courts. He concluded that a fine of £10, or twenty days imprisonment, would satisfy the ends of justice.

Needless to say, the cash was quickly handed over and Sir John, accompanied by his friends, left the court.

Beware – Card Sharks
A short piece in the Caledonian Mercury from 1854 is worth repeating in full.

'On Monday evening, at Linlithgow, three gamblers were turned out of one of the carriages of the Edinburgh and Glasgow for playing cards. A dupe in the same compartment had lost four pounds, and gave information, when the station-master gave orders to have the fellows expelled, which they at once were, although with

some difficulty. We are only surprised that such a stale trick could be successful at the present day, after all the warnings that have been given.'

Violent Assault
Source:
Caledonian Mercury, Thursday 30th January 1851

The punishment of outlawry seems to have been used increasingly rarely as the nineteenth century proceeded. A late example, for a Linlithgowshire man at least, was that of William Graham. On Monday 27th January 1851 he was accused, at the High Court of Justiciary, of assaulting John Corkle with a hammer, in his own house at Carniehead, Linlithgow, on the night of 28th to 29th September the previous year. Corkle lost a lot of blood, and nearly his life, but survived. Graham's failure to appear in court was taken as a confession of guilt and he was outlawed, as we have seen happen to a number of other non-appearers.

'Frightful Murder Near Bathgate' – Sectarian Violence in Linlithgowshire
Source:
Glasgow Herald, Friday 21st November 1856, Wednesday 14th January 1857 and Wednesday 4th February 1857
The Scotsman, Tuesday 3rd February 1857
Aberdeen Journal, Wednesday 9th April 1857

As was discussed at the opening of this chapter, the 1850s saw large numbers of people move into the south of the county. Many of these came from Ireland, from both sides of the sectarian divide. Against this backdrop it was inevitable that there would be trouble. In 1856, it boiled over into a murder which caught the public imagination, being widely reported in the newspapers. On 21st November the Glasgow Herald found the story so interesting that it carried two accounts – one from the Scotsman and one from the Falkirk Herald. On 14th January the following year it gave an account of the resulting trial, then, on 4th February, of the execution.

This account of the events of the night of Saturday 15th to Sunday 16th November 1856 are pieced together from the initial news stories and the account

92 | CHAPTER THREE

of the trial.

As there were a number of people involved a cast list might be helpful:

Peter McLean	Chief attacker
William Mansfield	Assistant attacker
Christina McLean	Wife of Peter
John Maxwell	Intended victim
Thomas Maxwell	Brother of John, actual victim
Edward McGlachan	Passer by
Neil McMullen	Rescuer
James Pollan	Rescuer
Sergeant Kerr	Police officer, called to the scene
Mary Kerr	Wife of the Sergeant

The men involved were colliers, employed in the pits of Messrs. Russel & Son, of Falkirk. As well as being workmates, they were neighbours, living in cottages at Durhamtown, about a mile from Bathgate. On the night in question, the Maxwell brothers, Thomas and John, were ambushed at Boghead, halfway between Bathgate and their home, by William Mansfield and Peter McLean. Initial press reports suggested that McLean's wife, Christina, may also have been involved. The Maxwells were Catholics while their attackers were described as Orangemen.

McLean had fallen out with John Maxwell:

'with whom he has had some difference regarding their views of religion'

... and was looking for an opportunity settle the score.

Saturday was pay day and McLean and Mansfield knew that the Maxwells had gone into Bathgate to receive their wages. In common with many miners in the vicinity, the Maxwells tended to celebrate in the Bathgate pubs on that night of the week. McLean was familiar with the brothers' routine and, abetted by his friend William Mansfield, he decided to ambush them on the way home. This was no heat-of-the-moment crime: McLean had purchased a knife in Bathgate that evening for use in the attack.

As Mansfield and McLean lay in ambush, with McLean's wife and daughter close by, they were seen by two or three parties passing along the road. The ambushers were also spotted by Edward McGlachan, another miner, who was visiting a friend in Durhamtown. On his way back to his home in Bathgate just after eleven, he passed the McLean party. He heard one man say *'I shall do for the _____ tonight'.* A woman replied *'Mind, do it sure and quietly'.* McGlachan carried on and passed the Maxwells shortly after, but didn't think to warn them!

After accosting at least one innocent passer by, whom they released somewhat ruffled but unhurt, their intended victims finally appeared. In his evidence, John Maxwell recalled that he and his brother had spent the evening in several public houses. The last one was Chalmers', which he remembered entering but not leaving, having *'got fuddled'.* When the Maxwells came into view their attackers struck, but got the wrong man: Thomas was killed – stabbed seven times, including a fatal blow through the heart. John dodged a knife blow from Peter McLean but Mansfield struck him on the back of the head with a stone or something similar. Knocked to the ground, he was slashed and kicked in the head so hard that his bloody hair was later found on his assailants' shoes.

Meanwhile, the noise of the fight had brought other people to the scene. Neil McMullen told the court that he had seen the Maxwells in a number of pubs that night and then in Patrick Devellin's house. He was still there when the Maxwells had set off for home. Shortly afterward, a woman dashed into the pub saying that there were shouts of murder on the road. McMullen went out and heard the shouts, coming from the road towards Durhamtown. He and another man, James Pollan, quickly ran towards the noise. Arriving, he saw Peter McLean on top of John Maxwell and Mansfield on top of Thomas. Christina McLean was stooping over John and her daughter was in the middle of the road shouting. McMullen heard Mansfield say, *'Come away, Pate, there's plenty harm done. Come away, there's somebody comin''.* McLean replied, *'I'll never leave him till I kill him.'* Mansfield was not prepared to wait and turned tail. McLean decided not to face the newcomers on his own and quickly followed.

McMullen and Pollan rushed up to the Maxwells. John Maxwell looked up and said, *'See how we're kilt and murdered.'* Thomas was still. McMullen said to John, *'Hold on till I catch them.'* Then they set off in pursuit. Pollan was already on his way and caught Mansfield. McMullen caught McLean and said to him, *'See how you've murdered the men.'* Mclean replied, *'I'll do it to you, too, if you don't let me go.'* McMullen told the court that he had knocked McLean down, and said, *'I'll watch you for that.'* Christina McLean came rushing up towards him and she and her husband managed to get away. Meanwhile, Mansfield had escaped from Pollan.

McMullen and Pollan held a quick conference and decided to go back to try and help the Maxwells. When they reached the site of the ambush they found that Thomas was dead and John had gone. When asked later, all that John could remember was coming round on his own and making his way home. When he got there, neighbours saw how injured he was and sent for a doctor, who came and stitched his wounds. McMullen and Pollan decided to go to Durhamtown to look for McLean and Mansfield, where they found that the alarm had already been raised, possibly by the arrival of John Maxwell.

We'll now turn to Sergeant Kerr. He had already seen at least one of the cast list that Saturday: at about 9pm he had seen Mrs McLean at Peter Russell's butcher shop in Bathgate, where she bought half a cow's head and some mutton. At a quarter past one in the morning he was alerted to the incident at Durhamtown and made his way there with one of his constables. He was met by McMullen, Pollan and other angry neighbours. They showed him Thomas Maxwell's body, then took him up to Mansfield's house. Gaining entry, Kerr placed Mansfield under arrest. Next they went to the McLeans' house, where they had to force entry. Sergeant Kerr described what he found there. Mrs McLean was still up, and drunk. Peter McLean was in bed but still dressed. He had blood on his trousers and his hands. With the help of the local vigilantes, he took Mansfield and the McLeans into Bathgate. McMullen recalled Christina McLean struggling with him and complaining that he should be on their side since he was from the same community in Ireland. In Bathgate, Sergeant Kerr examined his prisoners. He found that Peter McLean had blood on his face, neck and cap. The job of searching Christina he gave to his wife, Mary. As well as a bloody handkerchief, she found a knife, still wet with blood, in her pocket. Returning to the McLean's house, Kerr found Peter's boots, with blood and hair sticking to them, and a tub and a basin filled with water and blood. It seemed that some unsuccessful attempts had been made to clean themselves up. This gave rise to a statement in the Scotsman that they were caught *'in the very act of washing the blood from their hands'.* Just to be sure that none of this could have come from Christina's earlier shopping, Kerr checked the cow's head and found it to be still whole and free from blood stains.

The next day, Mansfield and the three McLeans were taken to Linlithgow prison. McLean's step daughter[6] was soon released, and on 12th January 1857 the other three were put on trial for murder and assault. The account above is drawn, largely, from the evidence of the prosecution witnesses. Of course, the accused were allowed to give their version of events. According to them, the Maxwell brothers, aided by McMullen, had been the aggressors. Other than that, their stories did not entirely tally. Mansfield said that he had run away from the fight, but that he had heard Peter say that he had something in his pocket which he would use if they did not let him alone. Peter denied carrying a knife and said that he had never seen the one found on his wife. Christina said that the blood had come from the cow's head, which she had been cutting before the police broke in, implying that it was just one of their kitchen knives.

The Lord Justice-Clerk summed up for the Crown. He thought it worth the jury considering whether all the accused were equally guilty. Christina McLean, was probably guilty of nothing more than assault while her husband had a very strong case against him for murder. Mansfield's case lay somewhere in between. He had clearly taken part in the assault and it was for the jury to decide if his involvement might be such as to make him guilty either of murder, or at least of being an accessory to it, meaning that he was complicit, and that without him the murder would not have taken place.

The jury took forty minutes to consider their verdicts. They found the case against Christina to be not proven. William Mansfield was found guilty of assault and Peter McLean was found guilty of murder.

After due consideration, Mansfield was given a sentence of two years hard labour. Subject to review by the Crown, the court had no choice but to sentence Peter McLean to death. He was to be held in Linlithgow Prison until 2nd February, being fed only on bread and water, and then executed between eight and ten in the morning. The sobbing prisoner was removed from the court.

The Crown saw no reason to be lenient and the execution was carried out as detailed by the judge. The Scotsman gave a lengthy account, which gives some idea of the interest in the murder and also the newsworthiness of a public execution.

On a hazy and raw Monday morning, at eight o'clock exactly, McLean was hung in the space between the front of the County Buildings and Cross Well. This was the first execution to be held in Linlithgow since that of Ralph Woodness back in 1819, 38 years earlier. In fact, the burgh scaffold had lain unused for so long that two months earlier the authorities had sold it to a baker in the town who had used it for firewood! As a result, they had had to borrow equipment from Edinburgh.

Due to the novelty value and the sectarian element, the authorities foresaw the possibility of a large number of spectators, and the potential for trouble. The

Railway Mania and the Birth of the Shale Industry

town started to fill up on the Sunday afternoon, with coach loads of miners arriving from far-flung parts of the county. All the local shops were instructed to stay shut until after the event was finished; indeed the pub owners had been told that they would lose their licence if they opened between 11pm on Saturday night and 11am on Monday. In practise, a smaller crowd than expected materialised – only three or four thousand, though a train load of miners arrived at 8:30am, having been deliberately misinformed of the time of the execution.

Two days earlier, to avoid transporting him down the High Street on the morning of the execution, McLean was transferred, with an escort of a detachment from the 5th Dragoon Guards, from the New Prison (which stood on the site which was to be home to the new Court House, beside the County Buildings) to the one remaining cell in the Burgh Halls. On the fateful morning, he is described as looking wretched, and as seeming weak and helpless, as well he might. He was pinioned and brought to the gallows by the executioner, in the company of two officers and the Reverend Doctor Bell, who ministered to him in his last days. His final words to the crowd were:

'Good people, take a warning by me. Avoid evil company and drink, and keep the Sabbath Day.'

He was dead within a minute.

To the end he maintained that if he had committed the crime he had no memory of it and had not intended it, while his wife, somewhat contradictorily, argued that:

'There is no doubt that Peter was guilty; but Mansfield was as bad as him, and should have got the same sentence.'

The Scotsman account gives an indication of how rare hangings were in Scotland at this time: the executioner, Mr Calcraft, had to be brought up from London, and his movements are described as minutely as those of the prisoner. He would seem to have had a certain ghoulish celebrity status.

Calcraft had left London on the preceding Thursday night, clearly by train, though this is not stated, and arrived in Edinburgh the next morning. From there he had travelled directly to Linlithgow:

'His presence soon, after becoming known, tended to increase the prevailing

Railway Mania and the Birth of the Shale Industry

excitement in the town.'

He kept out of sight over the weekend. Of course, no-one knew what he looked like, and the paper reports that:

'Not less, probably, than fifty harmless individuals were at various times pointed out as Mr Calcraft.'

Meanwhile, he was sitting in a skull-cap and slippers, smoking his pipe in apartments in the prison.

Not wanting to trust to whatever the provincials would provide, Calcraft travelled with his own rope, with a special hook, and pinioning straps. Clearly, he was a dedicated professional!

This case was to have one further consequence. The cost of the execution had been borne by the burgh of Linlithgow, and at a meeting of the Convention of Royal Burghs, held in Edinburgh in April 1857, the Linlithgow representative sought the support of his peers in calling for the transfer of responsibility for organising and paying for such events to the Crown. This led to a lively debate, and while some members supported the idea, others were concerned that this would erode the power of their magistracies. In the end, the majority voted in favour a compromise motion which sought to retain the duty to organise executions but to petition the Crown to pay.

McIver v McIver
Source:
Glasgow Herald, Monday 30th January 1860

This chapter began with some accounts of domestic abuse. A case from the end of its time frame also relates to this subject, though with a less tragic outcome.

In January 1860 Mrs Francis McIver took her husband James to the Court of Session. She had separated from him:

'on account of his having inflicted on her personal violence.'

James, who worked at the Kinneil Iron Works, had already been found guilty at the Sheriff Court in Linlithgow of beating her. In this second case she was seeking £26 in alimony. James didn't show up, or send a representative and as a result the Court granted her request:

'holding that when a reasonable ground for separation was alleged, and the husband did not come to Court to deny it, or to offer to take his wife back, the Court would not inquire into the amount of cruelty to determine whether or not is was such as to form sufficient ground for judicial separation.'

Is No-one Safe?
Source:
Caledonian Mercury, Wednesday 22nd August 1860

We will finish this chapter with a case that shows a shocking lack of respect for authority. It is notable that once again the villain was a miner, showing either how hard the lives of these men were, or that they were an immoral bunch, depending on your point of view!

'GARDEN THEFTS – Early on Sunday morning, Constables Rutherford and Broglan, of the Linlithgow constabulary, apprehended James Snadden, a miner, who had broken into the garden of the Rev. Kenneth Mackenzie, minister of Borrowstounness, and helped himself liberally to fruit. The fellow was caught in the act, and will, it is to be hoped, be suitably punished.'

Chapter Four: 1861-80 – The Height of Empire

The Height of the Empire

Introduction

The period from 1861 to 1880 saw the economic peak of Victorian Britain. Britain was a world power, and as a result events across the globe could have an impact upon its economy. The American Civil War disrupted the cotton trade, while conflicts in Europe, such as the Franco-Prussian War and the reunification of Italy, upset trade on the continent. To make matters worse, Britain was losing the technological lead it had gained in the early stages of the Industrial Revolution; France and the United States were catching up; and in 1871 a new power emerged on the scene with the unification of Germany. Markets became more competitive and profit margins became tighter: the situation was made harder for companies seeking to export their produce by many countries, including Britain, seeking to protect their industries through raising import tariffs. The result was that in 1873 the British economy went into what was to become known as the Long Depression, from which it would not emerge until 1896.

Scotland and Linlithgowshire were not immune from these events. Unemployment, and under-employment, became endemic as the business community sought to adapt to the new, harsher economic conditions. Not all industries suffered equally, however. At one end of the spectrum, shale mining continued to thrive, while at the other, the pressure on traditional crafts increased. In some ways though, this was a less volatile period than the decades before. After the influxes experienced during the building of the canal, the railways and the opening up of the shale mines, this was a period of relative population stability in the county and the country as a whole.

The approach to punishment altered markedly during this period. Penal Servitude Acts were passed in 1853 and 1857, paving the way for the phasing out of transportation and the more extensive use of incarceration as a means of punishment. The colonies were increasingly reluctant to accept convicts and there was a growing feeling in Britain that transportation was a waste of resources, inadequate as a punishment and ineffective as a deterrent. Though the last convict ship arrived in Western Australia as late as 1868, transportation was little used in the years leading up to that date. The extension of incarceration as a punishment required the construction of larger, centralised prisons in place of the network of local jails. Penal servitude subjected the prisoners to backbreaking hard labour on machines such as the treadmill and the crank. Both of these machines had the potential to produce energy which could be used productively, however it was easier, and thus more common, to set them up to be non-productive. The crank would be attached to a paddle inside a box filled with gravel, or something similar, and the inmate would be required to turn it 10,000 times each day. Prisoners began their sentences in solitary confinement and could gradually earn privileges, such as a mattress to sleep on or a reduced work load, through good behaviour. This is the reverse of today's approach where prisoners start off with rights which they may then lose through bad behaviour. The philosophy of the purpose of prisons had swung back in favour of retribution rather than rehabilitation. Recognising that this was a more intensive punishment regime, the tariffs were reduced. Instead of sentences of seven, fourteen and 21 years transportation the equivalent periods of penal servitude were five, ten and fifteen years.

In 1877 the Prisons Act brought all prisons under central government control, with responsibility north of the border being given to the newly created Prisons Commission for Scotland. 1880 saw work start on Barlinnie. In Linlithgow, the town built itself a new Sheriff Court House, which was opened in grand style in April 1865. An example of the national nature of the justice system came in 1878 when the head of the Isle of Man police force, David Monro, was appointed chief constable of the counties of Edinburgh and Linlithgow, filling the gap left by W. H. Stuart Johnston, who was taking on the position of Inspector of Prisons in Scotland.

She Fought the Law and the Law Won
Source:
Caledonian Mercury, Thursday 31st October 1861, Tuesday 17th December 1861 and Tuesday 10th June 1862

We have seen before that failure to appear for trial could result in the accused being outlawed. This sanction was used into the 1860s, at least. On Wednesday 30th October 1861 Linlithgow woman Bridget Kelly was a no-show at the High Court of Justiciary and suffered this penalty. She may have made a good decision as the judges seem to have been in a fairly severe mood that day. One Edinburgh man got eight years for stealing a pram, while another got four for stealing a ham. Her period of outlawry did not last long as on 16th December she was brought before the High Court.

She was charged with violently assaulting John Neally with a poker. Now Neally was a furnace filler in Kinneil, so one may presume that he was a fairly strong man, but attacked by Kelly and her poker he was badly injured, lost a lot of blood, and was considered to have been in some danger of losing his life. She pled

The Height of the Empire

not guilty, but after hearing the evidence the jury convicted her. Despite the seriousness of the attack, and her previous non-appearance, she escaped with a sentence of just six months.

At just around the time that Kelly would have been released a more traditional assault occurred in Whitburn. It was more traditional in that it was by a man on his wife.

Thomas Gay was a journeyman baker and he and his wife were incomers to Whitburn. According to the Caledonian Mercury journalist, they had not enjoyed a happy marriage, largely due to them both being *'addicted to habits of intemperance'.*

On the evening of Friday 6th June he was drunk, as usual, and in a violent mood. Witnesses reported that trouble had been brewing for some hours until, at about 9pm, he grabbed her and tried to manhandle her out of their upper storey flat. She resisted, he hit her hard, she lost her footing and fell down thirteen stairs to the passage below, her head striking the flagstones. Her skull was fractured and she was unconscious for twelve hours. Thomas was arrested and transferred to Linlithgow Prison. Mrs Gay was nursed in Whitburn where she was visited by the Sheriff. It proved to be a wasted trip as she was incapable of speech.

Absent Without Leave
Source:
Caledonian Mercury, Wednesday 22nd January 1862
Glasgow Herald, Friday 22nd August 1862

From 1820 onwards, the British Army had a trained reserve force in the form of local militias, an early form of the modern Territorial Army. This involved recruits undertaking basic training followed by an annual two week training camp. For the first forty years the regiments were solely infantry, but in 1861 some were trained as artillery. Of course, service was paid, and was taken seriously (at least by the authorities) as was shown by a case which came before Linlithgow Justice of the Peace Court on Monday 20th January 1862.

The case of William McKinlay was heard by Henry Temple Blair, Esq. McKinlay was a private in the Haddington, Berwick and Peebles Militia Artillery. He was charged with having missed training every year from 1858 to 61. Under the law, absence from training was to be treated as desertion, and the offender could either be tried in his regimental court or by any Justice of the Peace:

'in whose jurisdiction he may be found, as the Secretary of State for War may direct.'

Presumably he was living in, or arrested in, Linlithgowshire, since that is where he was tried.

McKinlay pled guilty and was sentenced to two months in prison or a fine of £2. He got off pretty lightly - the article concludes with a warning that:

'Militiamen would do well to bear in mind that by absenting themselves from the training of their corps, they are liable, upon conviction, to a penalty of £20, or six months imprisonment.'

The failure of men to show up was obviously a problem for the authorities, but militiamen could also find themselves in trouble for going too far the other way. It was illegal for militiamen to enlist in the regular army – a sort of military bigamy. Later in 1862, Bernard Crawson, a private in the 1st Royal Lanark Militia, was found to have fallen foul of this law and sentenced to one month's imprisonment.

'A Curious Case of Window-Breaking'
Source
Caledonian Mercury, Friday 29th August 1862
The Scotsman, Friday 29th August 1862

Prison is, of course, intended to act as a punishment and a deterrent. However, there are times when imprisonment is seen as a better option than the alternatives. In the nineteenth century, prison life was a lot harder than today, but so too could life be on the streets. On the evening of Tuesday 26th August 1862 a man called William Gallacher, who appeared to be a tramp, was seen to lift a large stone off the street and throw it through the window of James Aitken's baker shop in Hopetoun Street in Bathgate. The window, which was estimated to be worth nearly £3 by the Caledonian Mercury but just £2 10s by the Scotsman, was completely shattered. Standing a few metres away was a police constable. He arrested Gallacher, who made no effort to escape. On being questioned, he:

'frankly admitted that he had broken the glass wilfully, in order that he might get into prison'.

The Height of the Empire

He explained that he was a shoemaker by trade but had been unable to find work for three months, despite travelling across country in his search, and was literally starving for lack of food. On seeing the policeman, it had occurred to him that if he broke the window he could get himself arrested.

Clothes Theft
Source:
Caledonian Mercury, Saturday 4th October 1862

Earlier in the century (see 'A Day in the High Court 1838', for example) we saw people being transported for relatively minor thefts. The difference in sentencing at this period is clear in the case of Mary Murdoch, or McKenna, who also went by the aliases of Morton or McCann. She pled guilty to stealing:

'several articles of wearing apparel from a locked drawer, in a house at Linlithgow, in September last.'

Not only had she committed this theft but she had three previous convictions for theft. A generation earlier she would have been sentenced to seven years transportation, but in the more enlightened regime in 1862 she was given six months imprisonment.

The Winchburgh Train Disaster

Part 1. The Crash
Source:
The Scotsman, Tuesday 14th October 1862
Glasgow Herald, Wednesday 15th October 1862 (quoting a number of sources),
Thursday 16th October and Monday 5th January 1863

Sometimes the name of a little known town becomes synonymous with a calamitous event. For many years, the name of Winchburgh was known in connection with the rail disaster of Monday 13th October 1862.

The basic facts are simply stated: two trains were put onto the same track and crashed head-on. The details are more complicated, as was the search for an explanation.

At 6pm that evening, a passenger train left Edinburgh for Perth comprising two third class carriages, two first class carriages, a van and a horse box. It reached Ratho at about 6:15 and then headed on to its next stop at Linlithgow.

Coming in the opposite direction was the 5pm passenger train from Glasgow, which had seven carriages. This train was unusually busy, transporting many people back from a day at the Falkirk Tryst. Indeed, there seems to have been standing room only from the time it left Glasgow. It passed through Linlithgow without incident.

Since 15th September, engineering works had been taking place on the line just west of Winchburgh and as a result there was a stretch of track a little over two miles long in a deep, narrow cutting where there was only a single line in operation. Both trains were directed onto this line at the same time and at about 6:30 they crashed head on.

The drivers saw each other's trains a few seconds before impact. Both managed to put on their brakes, as was confirmed by the accident investigators, but to little avail. The driver of the Glasgow train managed to fling himself from his engine just before impact and survived, though badly injured. The driver of the train from Edinburgh was not so lucky.

The scene was described by eyewitnesses in the most heart-rending terms. The two engines and their tenders were smashed to pieces, as was each train's leading (third class) carriage. Other carriages were piled up (according to some accounts, as high as a three storey building) or strewn across the area. The wounded and dying cried and groaned while trapped passengers shrieked and screamed. Mercifully, the rear coaches were largely undamaged, though their passengers did not all escape from injury as they slammed to a halt.

News of the accident quickly reached Winchburgh and Linlithgow and people hastened to the scene to give what help they could. Linlithgow's Sheriff Cay had been travelling in the train from Glasgow and had escaped unhurt. He and Provost Dawson (who was quickly on the scene) helped to organise the efforts to rescue survivors from the carriages and tend to the injured.

A telegram was sent to Edinburgh requesting medical assistance and a special train was sent out, bringing four doctors to join the one from Winchburgh and four from Linlithgow who were already on the spot. The doctors found some people beyond hope and others who required immediate attention. Edinburgh

The Height of the Empire

Royal Infirmary was contacted with instructions to send stretchers and make beds ready. Many people had broken limbs, some so mangled that they required amputation. The boiling water from the engines had severely scalded several passengers.

Most of the injured were put into still functioning first class carriages and slowly and carefully taken back to Edinburgh, arriving at about 10pm. Word had gone round the city like wildfire and Waverley Station was crowded with anxious friends and relatives, as well as people drawn by ghoulish fascination. A number of the victims were transported in the other direction, to Linlithgow.

While survivors took priority, the painful job of recovering the dead also had to be undertaken. Amazingly, only twelve people had been killed at the scene. Sadly, five more died of their injuries within twenty four hours.

Part 2. The Search For Answers
Source:
Glasgow Herald, Thursday 16th October 1862 and Monday 5th January 1863
Caledonian Mercury, Tuesday 17th February 1863

Even as work continued to clear the line and tend to the injured, investigations were begun into the causes of the crash. The following morning, 47 year old points operator George Newton was taken into custody by the Linlithgowshire police, examined by Sheriff Home and charged with culpable homicide and neglect of duty. Much was made in the court and the press of George Newton's inexperience as a pointsman. He had recently returned to the railway after a spell as a ploughman and had been hastily allocated to this key role when another pointsman had made it clear that he intended to quit. Newton was the man who had allowed the train from Glasgow onto the line, and was therefore the person who could most easily be thought to be at fault. However, it soon became clear that the responsibility lay with more than one person and an inquiry was set up by the Lords of the Committee of Privy Council for Trade under Captain Tyler, R.E. He reported back to them on 30th October.

During the engineering works, the procedure was supposed to be that any train going onto the single track section would be accompanied by a pilot engine, which would follow 400 yards behind. A crucial element in the case was that the normal, distinctive, pilot engine had been taken out of service for repairs and temporarily replaced with a larger engine not normally used for such work. Entry onto the single track section was managed by two pointsmen, stationed at each end to control entry into the section, through standard railway signals. It seems that, over the weeks, a certain slackness had crept in. Especially during daylight, the pilot engine wasn't always used to escort trains through, and in fact it was sometimes utilised to shunt the odd wagon or to move workmen along the line. Those involved knew the timetable pretty well and it was normal for the 6pm from Edinburgh to go through the section before the 5pm from Glasgow, though sometimes the latter managed to get through first. Trains were supposed to enter the single track section at a maximum of 4mph and to traverse it carefully, but the drivers became confident and got into the habit of accelerating once they were on it. All-in-all, it seems as if things had got pretty sloppy.

On the night of the accident, the main source of confusion seems to have come because a goods train, followed by an engine which resembled the stand-in pilot engine, was allowed to go onto the line at the eastern end without the accompaniment of the actual pilot. This engine was pulling a wagon and an old coach, which should have helped to identify it as not being the pilot engine, but as we have seen, the pilot was often used in this kind of work. To further add to the confusion, the driver of this engine had gone into a siding on exiting the single track section, just as the pilot engine would do. In fact, it was simply getting out of the way, knowing that the much faster train from Edinburgh could not be far behind. Newton mistakenly thought that this was the pilot and that the line was therefore clear. The accounts of surviving staff from the train from Glasgow confirmed that they had made the same mistake, showing that this was not pure inexperience or lack of attention on his part. There seemed no reason for him to hold back the train from Glasgow so he signalled it to proceed. Meanwhile, the train from Edinburgh had been allowed on, as the pointsman at the east end expected the train from Glasgow to wait until it was through, as usually happened.

Captain Tyler was damning in his criticism of those involved and made a number of recommendations for changes to railway procedures. It was clear that blame lay at a higher level than the individual pointsmen and the eyes of the authorities turned to those in positions of responsibility.

Part 3. The Trial of Mr Latham and Mr Thomson
Source:
Glasgow Herald, Saturday 7th February 1863 (from The Courant) and Wednesday 18th February 1863
Caledonian Mercury, Tuesday 17th February 1863

The Height of the Empire

John Latham was the general manager of the Edinburgh and Glasgow Railway and James Boyd Thomson was the superintendant of traffic on the line. They were the men whom the authorities concluded bore the responsibility for the crash. Latham was charged with culpable homicide and Thomson with neglect of duty, leading to the deaths and injuries of a number of staff and passengers. It was held to be their job to ensure that proper procedures were in place at the engineering works and that they were followed. The trial date was set at Monday 16th February 1863 and 49 witnesses were called. Such was the public interest that the account of the trial took up nearly two pages in the broadsheet Caledonian Mercury.

Proceedings began at 10am, before the Lord Justice-Clerk, Lord Ardmillan and Lord Jerviswoode. The prosecution case was led by the Lord Advocate and his deputy while Latham and Thomson each had two counsels: this was high-powered stuff.

The first area of discussion was around the instructions which had been issued to the men working in the area. The prosecution argued that they were not sufficiently detailed and rigorous. For example, it was company policy that the driver of a pilot train was supposed to wear a red cap, to allow him to be easily recognised, but this had not been specified in the instructions issued by Thomson, which were approved by Latham, at the outset of the work in September. The author of the report to the Privy Council, Captain Tyler, was examined and identified a number of other areas where the instructions were insufficiently detailed, or ill advised. One example of the latter was that he felt that a pilot-man would have been safer than a pilot engine. That is to say, a train would not be allowed to go onto the single track section unless the pilot-man was on board.

A number of officials from the railway were called to give evidence, as were a number of staff involved in the events, including both pointsmen and the driver of the Glasgow train. A lot of questions were asked about the process whereby safety instructions were instituted and who could alter them. A picture emerged in which a number of people had input into the instructions and no one person could really be said to have complete responsibility. The Glasgow Herald summed up the situation nicely:

'In the first place, it is evident that the regulations imposed by the Directors of the Edinburgh and Glasgow Railway are so very indefinite that nobody seems to be responsible or to blame for anything. Mr. Latham is supposed to be Manager, and

yet Mr. Adie, the Engineer of the line, is positively declared to be an independent functionary. Mr. Jamieson, the Secretary, thinks that Mr. Thomson "can be controlled by Mr. Latham," but he is evidently not very sure; while Mr. Dunlop, Vice-chairman of the Company, seems to think that the Secretary, the Manager, and the Engineer are three separate and independent powers, subject only to the supreme control of the Directors. With such a constitution of authority, it is no wonder that the saddle cannot be placed upon the right horse.'

After several hours of evidence of this nature, the Lord Advocate, who it will be remembered was leading the prosecution, decided enough was enough. He addressed the court to say that he was withdrawing the charges against Latham and Thomson. He had become convinced that there were substantial problems with the safety regulations of the railway and of their operation, but that the blame for this lay at many doors and that it would not be right to take action against these two particular men. The Lord Justice-Clerk instructed the jury to find the accused not guilty, which they duly did, and the case was concluded.

Part 4. Further Court Actions
Source:
Caledonian Mercury, Saturday 28th February 1863 and Tuesday 1st September 1863
Glasgow Herald, Saturday 11th July, 1863, Friday 31st July 1863 and Saturday 1st August 1863
Birmingham Daily Post, Tuesday 4th August 1863

The collapse of the trial against Latham and Thomson did not, of course, bring matters to a close: people were dead and injured and even if no-one was going to go to jail the railway company could not deny its overall responsibility. In the immediate aftermath of the crash they made a large number of settlements to the victims, or their bereaved, but a number of individuals took the company to court, demanding large sums of compensation money. These cases were to drag on for the best part a year, keeping the disaster in the public eye.

To start with, the railway took on a bullish, business as usual, persona. In February 1863 they were reporting good profits and a dividend to shareholders of 6%. Throughout the summer of 1863 a series of compensation cases came before the courts. Two interesting cases were those of Mrs Joanna Hedderwick and Mr Henry Welsh.

Mrs Joanna Hedderwick
Mrs Hedderwick claimed damages of £3,000 for the death of her 42 year old son,

The Height of the Empire

Falkirk solicitor Alexander Hedderwick. Her case came before the High Court of Justiciary on 10th July 1863. Her counsel asserted that the culpability of the railway company was not in question and that the point of the trial was to give the jury an appreciation of the amount of suffering and sorrow she had been caused, as well as its financial impact on her.

Adam Colquhoun, Chief Constable of Linlithgow, was called to describe the scene that night, and how he had found Alexander's body. George Newton was forced to relive the events yet again. Henry Welsh, a survivor who still had to walk with a crutch, described his experiences.

Two of the deceased's brothers, and two of his sisters, told the court how Alexander had been financially supporting his 75 year old mother and two unmarried sisters since the family business (inherited by another brother) had collapsed in 1861. The ladies were now reduced to such a condition that they had had to take in a lodger. Tragically for the family, Alexander's business had been making good progress and he had been talking about the possibility of bringing his mother and sisters to live with him before too long.

Summing up for the prosecution, the Lord Advocate thought that the jury would agree that:

'the accident was caused by the plainest, the most reprehensible, and the most unaccountable negligence, not on the part of the miserable pointsman, but in regard to the general arrangements, for which the company itself was clearly responsible.'

He could not conceive of a more discreditable case of negligence for the public safety and urged the jury to give the much-suffering Mrs Hedderwick a good settlement.

For the defence, the Solicitor-General stated that the railway had never disputed liability – the question for the jury was what represented fair compensation. He urged them to think of the railway's shareholders, who were made poorer by every pound paid out, many of them old ladies, old men and children who depended on receiving their dividends! He calculated that Alexander was giving his mother about £1 a week, and that if he had been paying that much into the life insurance contract it would have paid out something like £300 to £400. In his opinion, this would be a fair payout.

The jury, not surprisingly, took a middle course. After considering the case for twenty minutes they found in favour of Mrs Hedderwick and awarded damages of £1,750.

Mr Henry Welsh

Henry Welsh was a 38 year old clothier from Frederick Street in Edinburgh. His claim for £5,000 for the injuries he had sustained was heard in the Court of Session on Thursday 30th and Friday 31st July 1863. The case is interesting for the eyewitness description he gave.

As usual, the prosecution began by demonstrating the culpability of the railway company with the usual witnesses, such as George Newton and Archibald Neil (the driver of the train from Glasgow) called on to relive the events yet again. Mr Welsh was then called to relate his experiences as recorded by a journalist:

'I had occasion to go to Perth on 13th October last. I proceeded onwards towards Winchburgh in the second carriage from the engine. I was sitting on the centre of the seat, with my back to the engine. My face was knocked against the iron rod which passes up the centre of the carriage. I did not feel the shock at the time at all. The first thing I found when I came to my senses – I was alone among the debris of the broken carriages. I was not able to move myself from the position I was in, being jammed amongst the broken carriage. My face was bleeding at the time, but I cannot say I was suffering much pain. I kept calling out, and a gentleman came and took the broken carriages out of the way. After I got out I suffered dreadful pain from my broken leg. The gentleman laid me across a carriage seat on my back. It was a very dark and stormy night, and I was very cold. I lay about three hours that way, and then I was put into a van, brought to Edinburgh, and conveyed in a cab to my own house.

Soon after my arrival a doctor was sent for, and by chance Dr. Handyside was found. He came that night, and continued with me afterwards. He set my broken bone. The leg was broken at the top of the thigh. I was injured at the back of the knee of the same leg, and was bruised all over my body. On the right leg there were some puncture wounds. I suffered great pain in the face from my upper jaw-bone being fractured, and after a while four large abscesses formed in my face. I was confined to a lying position for eight weeks, and with lying the skin came off from my ankles right up.'

Welsh went on to describe his long and painful convalescence, part of which involved being sent to Bridge of Allan for his health. At the time of the trial, nine months after the crash, he was still unable to walk without a crutch. A number of doctors, including Handyside, were questioned on the state of Welsh's health and

The Height of the Empire

the extent to which he could hope to recover. They concurred that he might be able to undertake shop work but not the travelling which had formed his side of the business. To further demonstrate the seriousness of his condition, Welsh had, earlier that month, applied to Scottish Widows for life insurance. This application was refused and the secretary of the Widows was called to explain why.

The final set of defence witnesses, including Welsh's business partner, gave evidence showing that their business had suffered greatly in his absence, making a case for compensation based on the financial impact of his injuries.

The prosecution now produced a doctor of their own, Professor Syme, who concluded that Welsh was well on the mend and would soon be as right as rain, though with one leg an inch and a half shorter than the other. Calling him proved to be an error: three weeks earlier, the Professor had given a similarly upbeat report in the case of another of the victims, Mr Shaw[7], who had been bedridden since the accident and was also pursuing the railway company. The prosecution counsel was able to reveal that Shaw had in fact died the previous day, just after hearing that his claim of £6,000 had been reduced by the court to £2,000). This allowed them to discredit Professor Syme as an expert witness. It is impossible to tell to what extent the evident underestimation of the seriousness of Shaw's injuries influenced the jury in Welsh's case, but they came back with an award for Welsh of £3,000, the largest that any of the victims was to receive.

By the end of the summer, the finances of the railway company had been sorely dented, something which may have hastened amalgamation with the North British Railway in 1865. Two other cases worth mentioning are those of Mr Elder (a commercial traveller), who claimed £3,000 for the injuries he sustained and was awarded £1,800, and the tragic case of Eliza Gibb, who was eight months pregnant at the time of the crash and lost her child. She claimed for £1,000 but settled out of court for £250 plus £150 costs. The half year accounts published on 31st August 1863 showed that the company had paid out £27,366 5s 6d to claimants, almost wiping out their profits for the period: the remaining £1,503 would not have been enough to pay out one more serious claimant. With the death of Mr Shaw, the crash had claimed twenty lives plus Eliza Gibb's unborn child.

The amalgamated railway was to prove no more generous in the payment of damages, causing outrage at its treatment of the injured and bereaved following the Tay Bridge Disaster in 1879.

THE HEIGHT OF THE EMPIRE

Cattle Plague
Source:
Caledonian Mercury, Thursday 1st February 1866

The slaughtering of herds and the control of movement of animals were commonplace in the early years of the twenty first century as a series of epidemics broke out across Scotland. A story from early 1866 shows us that this was nothing new. With cattle plague spreading through the countryside, restrictions were put in place in the south east of Scotland. A number of men chose to ignore them, with the scale of the problem being demonstrated by one day's proceedings in the Justice of the Peace Court in Edinburgh.

First up was Alex Seton, a man of whom better would have been expected as the deputy lieutenant of Linlithgowshire. He pled guilty to driving 39 sheep from his farm (Preston) to Edinburgh. In his defence he said that he hadn't known that the controls applied to sheep. He was fined £5 plus costs.

George Somerville, a farmer at Prestonmains was found guilty of burying cattle which had died from rinderpest at too shallow a depth (the minimum was five feet), and without an adequate amount of quicklime. He was fined £20 plus costs.

George Tait, a flesher (butcher), pled guilty to buying six live sheep at the Edinburgh cattle market and driving them out to his home in Gorebridge. He was fined £2 plus costs.

Another flesher, D. Walkinshaw of Parkfoot in Berwickshire, also pled guilty to the charge of driving some fat sheep (the journalist's description!) from Pathfoot to Dalkeith, for which he was fined £5 plus costs.

A third flesher, Thomas Borthwick from Ratho, pled guilty to driving a bullock from New Mains Farm along the public road to Ratho. Like Walkinshaw, he was fined £5 plus costs.

The Height of the Empire

Above: Police photograph of Janet Walker (or Cunningham) of Linlithgow, convicted in 1880 of receiving stolen property. This picture, and the image on the following page of John McLure, come from the 'Linlithgowshire Rogue's Gallery', a scrapbook of mug shots compiled by the Edinburgh Police over a period of around 30 years from the 1870s onwards. Janet's case is on p130 and John's is on p118.

116 | Chapter Four

THE HEIGHT OF THE EMPIRE

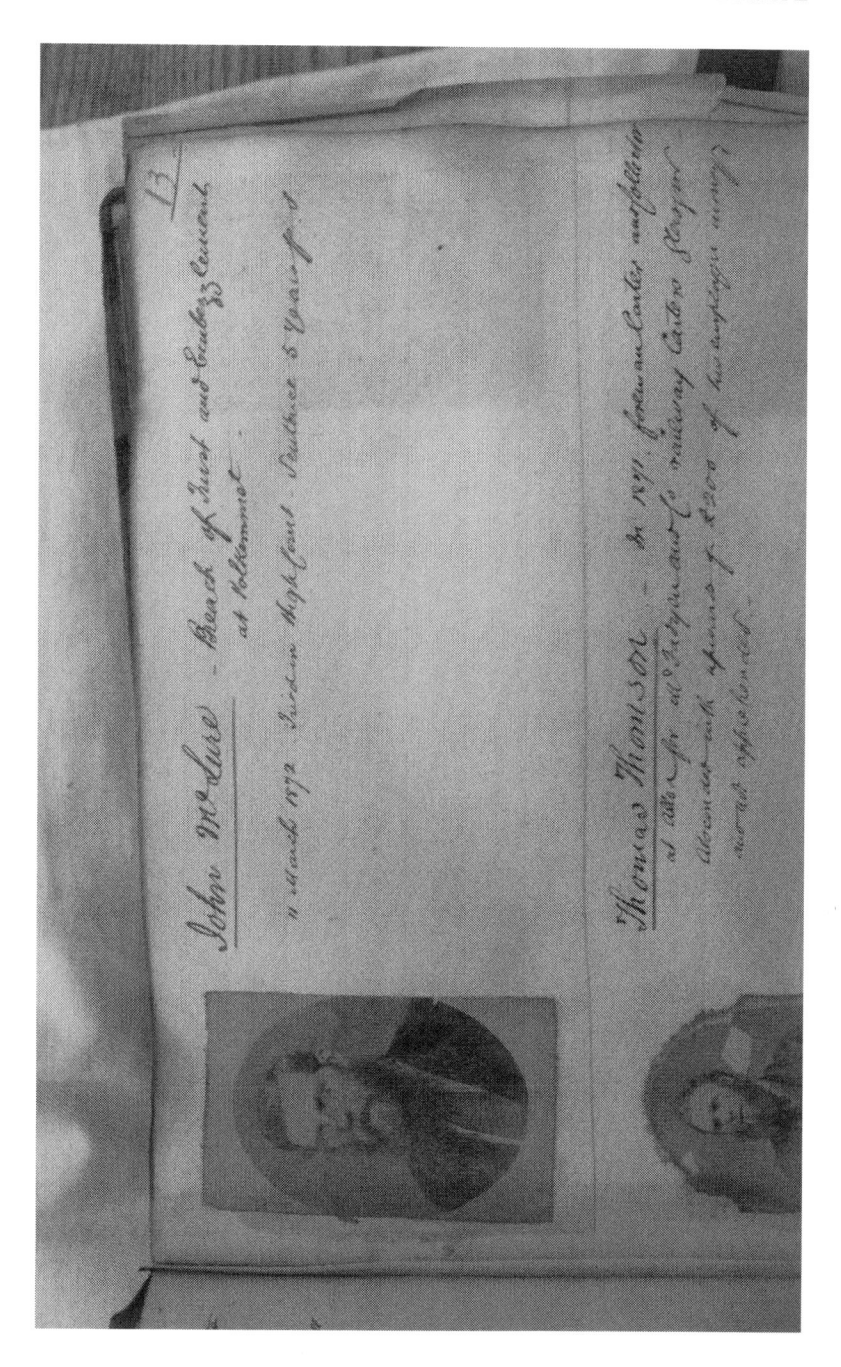

CHAPTER FOUR | 117

The Height of the Empire

Embezzlement
Source:
Glasgow Herald, Tuesday 12th March 1872

The story of John McLure is a sad one, showing how one error of judgement could result in many years of hard work being destroyed.

McLure (pictured on previous page) had started work at the Shotts Iron Company as a young lad of fourteen or fifteen. Over the course of the next sixteen years he worked his way up from the bottom rung to a senior position as the cashier in charge of the wages for staff at the company's sites at Polkemmet, Arden and Brownieside. This meant that as much as £2,000 could pass through his hands each month. His employers found that he was good at the job, and kept very accurate, careful records of all the money. Then, in June 1870, disaster struck. The newspaper record simply states that while travelling home one night in the train he lost a sum of the company's money. It is unclear if he was robbed, mislaid it or lost it through gambling to the sort of card sharks we saw being warned about back in 1851. Whatever the reason, he found himself faced with a dilemma. He considered coming clean, but decided that he would try and conceal the loss and gradually pay it back. Sadly, his efforts to recoup the losses backfired and he got into greater and greater trouble. As the black hole grew over the next year, he began to despair and became careless in his accounting, which inevitably led to the company becoming aware of the embezzlement. Finding out that he had been discovered, McLure fled the area, but after two months on the run he turned himself in to the authorities in October 1871. After five months in prison he came before the High Court of Justiciary where he was sentenced to five years penal servitude.

Toll Evasion
Source:
Glasgow Herald, Friday 14th June 1872

Road pricing is an old idea. Indeed, across the country many roads were built, or improved, through private investment, with the money being recouped through the charging of tolls. On Thursday 13th June two Edinburgh carters, William Bryce and Hugh Binnie, appeared at Linlithgow Sheriff Court charged with forcing open the toll-bar at Upper Kirkliston. Justice was swift in this case as the crime had only occurred on the 11th, two days earlier. The two men admitted forcing the toll-bar, and avoiding paying duty on their two horses and carts. Sheriff-Substitute Home fined them £1, with 10s of expenses, with the alternative of a month in prison. They went to prison.

The Uphall Wife Killers
Source:
Caledonian Mercury, Monday 19th November 1866
The Scotsman, Tuesday 20th November 1866 & Tuesday 4th February 1873
Glasgow Herald, Tuesday 4th February 1873 & Wednesday 5th February 1873

As we have seen, there were times when the High Court of Justiciary was called upon to decide where the line lay between murder and culpable homicide. Two cases from Uphall dating to 1866 and 1872 required juries to exercise their judgement in this way.

The first of the cases was heard on Monday 19th November 1866. The accused was a 44 year old itinerant basket maker named James Williamson. On 23rd May that year, he and his wife, Isabella, 37, were in Uphall, having travelled out the previous day from Edinburgh. The morning had passed with him doing a little basket making, her hawking them round the village, and the pair of them drinking heavily. As they were sitting by the side of the road with their two children they got into a quarrel and James, who was cutting bread, threw the contents of a jug of tea in Mary's face. She freed her arms from her shawl and squared up to him, hit him in the face with a piece of bread and then tried to run off. James followed, caught her up, kicked her leg and stabbed her in the chest with his knife. One witness reported that James had spoken of his wife's pugilistic abilities, and how he had come to blows with her on a number of occasions.

Isabella was not immediately incapacitated. Turned away from one neighbouring house she was given entry to another, where she asked only to be allowed to sit quietly and smoke her pipe. However, she was taken away for medical attention by a policeman who had been called to the scene. While a doctor carried out an examination, efforts were made to find her lodgings. As no-one in the vicinity was able or willing to put her up she was transferred to the stable of the local inn. The next day a good Samaritan, in the shape of a Mrs Grady, came forward and gave Isabella a bed for her remaining days.

It was a fairly shallow wound, only an inch deep, but it was to prove fatal with the poor woman dying ten days later. A doctor and a surgeon who had tended to her in her last days were examined in court. They gave evidence that her wound would not have killed her had she been healthy but the problem was that she had a weak constitution which had led to complications. How inconsiderate of her! For their part, the defence raised questions as to whether or not Isabella's death was caused by the wound or the treatment she received afterwards, including the night in the stable and the fact that she had then had to walk to Mrs Grady's house. So, was this murder or just a brutal assault which was just one of a number of factors which had contributed to the unfortunate woman's death? Sufficient doubt had entered the minds of the jurors. Having deliberated for a full five minutes they opted for manslaughter. Spared from the gallows, Williamson was sentenced to fifteen years penal servitude.

The second case was heard on Monday 3rd February 1873. The accused was George Farrie, who was charged with the murder of his wife, Catherine, on the night of 21st to 22nd October of the previous year, on the road between Uphall and Ecclesmachan. George was a 38 year old man. He had spent nineteen years in the army as a sapper and since being discharged had worked as a miner. He and Catherine had been married for thirteen years. They had had six children of whom only two were still alive – a fact which shows how brutal life could be at this time.

The Farries were well known to the innkeepers of the town. Both had problems with alcohol but Catherine's seem to have been more serious. The wife of a local publican described her as being very much addicted to drinking and related that when she was on a bender she and her clothes became dirty and unkempt. George had forbidden the local pubs from serving her, which they seem to have agreed to. Sometimes, in desperation, Catherine would forge a note from him for bottles of alcohol. George himself had a reputation for occasional overindulgence, rather than outright alcoholism. Not surprisingly, their relationship was a tempestuous one and they had separated temporarily during the preceding year, but had subsequently made up.

On the night of the 21st they had been out drinking together in a number of pubs and as last orders approached Catherine was visibly staggering. However, they seemed to be getting on well and picked up a bottle of whisky to take home, a journey which took them along the road, past a pond and across a field. For what happened next we only have George's account.

According to him, he and Catherine had not argued that night. He agreed that they were both drunk, and in the wet conditions that rainy night Catherine fell over several times. When they reached the pond they both fell over in the road. He got up and made his way home through the field. He went in to their house, knocked up the fire and warmed himself. After some time, when Catherine hadn't appeared, he went to look for her. After a brief search, he found her lying face down, part of the way across the field. He got her to her feet and they walked a short way when she fell over again. Realising that she wasn't capable of walking, he picked her up and carried her to their house. She kept saying how cold she was and he tried to warm her by putting her beside the fire, and sharing some of the whisky with her.

At its best, this account was unflattering to both parties. At its worst, it was unconvincing and failed to tally in a number of significant ways with the evidence that was given by other witnesses.

The next person to see the Farries was a neighbour, Anne Cunningham. She had turned in early that night but was woken at about half past twelve by George, pleading with her to come with him. She refused and he went away only to come back soon after and suffer a second rebuff. When he came for the third time he was crying bitterly and she agreed to go to their house. According to her, George said that he and Catherine had quarrelled on the way home and that she wanted to see Anne.

When they got to the house, Anne found that it was almost in darkness, illuminated only by the glow of the fire. She lit a lamp and saw Catherine slumped in a chair by the bed, covered in what was described as a pair of *'polkas'*. Anne took her hand and found it was very cold. She put her hand on Catherine's heart to try to feel for a pulse and realised that, under the polkas, she was naked. She asked George where Catherine's clothes were and he said he didn't know. She got George to carry Catherine to the fireside and when she was able to see her better she realised that she was wet, muddy and dead. When she gave George her medical opinion he said, *'Whisht; there's life in there yet,'* and tried to revive her by slapping her cheek, but to no effect. Anne demanded to know what had happened and he told her about leaving her in the road and then going back for her later. In this version of events, he said that he had found her in the pond itself. Anne sent George to fetch a doctor while she found some clothes to cover up the body.

Dr Skinner of Uphall was woken by George at shortly before 2am. George told him that something serious had happened, and persuaded him to go to their house. Dr Skinner confirmed that, as Anne had thought, Catherine was dead, and

The Height of the Empire

had probably been so for about an hour. Of course, he wanted to find out why and examined the body. As described in the indictment, he found her to have been brutally beaten: her body was a mass of wounds. He concluded that she had been punched many times in the face, on other parts of her head, as well as on her back and other areas of the body, and had then been beaten with a stick, cutting her in so many places that she had bled to death. He was quite clear that she had not drowned.

Local policeman, Constable Sangster, was soon on the case. Despite the doctor's findings, George told the Constable that his wife had drowned. In a piece of deduction worthy of the great Holmes, Sangster told the court that he felt:

'convinced that violence had been used.'

Not only that, but he suspected George, and told him as much! George was not willing to go quietly: he tried to escape and Sangster had to manacle him, hand and foot.

When day dawned, Sangster went to examine the field, assisted by Anne Cunningham. There, he found three areas where it looked as if there had been a fight, with trampled stubble, churned up soil, and pieces of Catherine's mud and blood spattered clothing. Putting all the evidence together, a picture emerged of an attack, ranging across the field, in which Catherine had been beaten horrifically, stripped of her clothes, dragged along the ground and pushed, or thrown, into the pond.

As far as the court was concerned there was only one suspect. As in the Williamson case, there was a strong argument that the assailant had not intended to kill his wife, and once again the jury came back with a verdict of culpable homicide. The difficult nature of the case is shown by the ninety minutes they took to reach a conclusion. The next day the court handed George Farrie the same sentence as James Williamson had received: fifteen years penal servitude.

That Williamson was guilty, there seems no doubt. However, in the Farrie case it is possible that there was a miscarriage of justice. If George left his wife lying in the road, dead drunk, in the early hours of a wet morning then that was appalling. If his story seemed to change in key particulars then that may have been due to the fact that he, too was pretty drunk that night, or that he was making unsuccessful attempts to make things look less bad for him. No one saw the assault and so it could be true that he did leave her and that she was attacked, possibly sexually, by someone else. One small piece of evidence suggests that we may allow there to be an element of doubt: everyone agreed that George had been wearing dark clothes on the 21st, so he cannot have been the man in white clothes that a further witness, John Brodie, saw leaving the field at about the right time that night. However, his evidence was not followed up and George took the blame, guilty or not.

'Assault By a Jealous Shoemaker'
Source:
Glasgow Herald, Tuesday 21st November 1872

How do you prove if a criminal is insane or not? Under the headline 'Assault By a Jealous Shoemaker', the Glasgow Herald told of the trial of Thomas West at the High Court of Justiciary on Monday 20th November 1872.

West and his lodger, Samuel Bennett, were both shoemakers, the most common profession for men living in Linlithgow at this time. West was a troubled man and had been drinking heavily in the week leading up to the 16th August. That night, he accused Bennett of being too familiar with his wife. Bennett seems to have been able to pacify him and went to work at William Watt & Son the next morning as normal. West also went to his work but was brooding over the wrong he believed had been done to him. He decided he couldn't let things lie until the end of the working day and started to walk out of the workshop. Understandably, his colleagues asked him where he was going, to which he replied that he meant to let some person see the face of his hammer. He walked into Watt's workshop, right up to Bennett and hit him twice on the head with said tool. Another of Watt's shoemakers tried to intervene and Bennett tried to make his escape. West threatened to run the workmate through with a knife and went in pursuit of Bennett. He caught up with his victim on a back stair and cut him on the lip and the left ear before a neighbour was able to rescue him.

West does not seem to have made any attempt to evade capture and was quickly arrested. The police constable reported that West seemed very cool and collected when he was arrested, and only wanted to know if he had managed to kill Bennett, making it clear that this had been his intention.

During his period in Linlithgow Prison the local physician, Dr Baird, had several conversations with him. Given that West had invoked a special defence of insanity the doctor's view on his mental state was highly significant. Though

Baird concluded that West suffered from jealous delusions he was not prepared to go so far as to say that he was insane. As a result, West was found guilty and sentenced to seven years penal servitude.

Breach of Promise
Source:
Trewman's Exeter Flying Post, Wednesday 22nd September 1875

It was somewhat unusual for a Linlithgowshire case to be reported in the pages of Trewman's Exeter Flying Post. However, one such occurrence was on Wednesday 22nd September, between a report of the trial of a Folkestone curate for *'Ritualistic practices'* and an item on the estimated cost of repairs at Lichfield Cathedral.

The case, heard at Linlithgow Sheriff Court, was brought by Mary Cairns, a domestic servant working in Haddington, against Thomas Morris, a miner from Armadale. The journalist explained that Armadale was near Bathgate, which may have been of limited help to an Exeter readership. Cairns was portrayed as a pretty girl of about nineteen, while the description of Morris was that he:

'is to appearance about twenty-six years of Age.'

They had met two years earlier, in the house of Mary Cairns' sister in Armadale. Just ten days later Morris wrote to her saying that if she was not already engaged, he would take her for his wife, and make her as happy as a queen. He had obviously made an equally good impression on her because she quickly wrote back, accepting his offer. In the words of the journalist, a loving correspondence followed, of which some details were provided to the court. In a letter dated 7th October he wrote that if God spared him then they would be as happy as a king and queen. In a later letter, in which he was seeking her advice on wedding arrangements, he concluded by saying: *'We will both be as happy as the day is long'*. Finally, they fixed on 31st December for their wedding. Everything seemed to be going well and in mid November Cairns came through to Armadale, at Morris's request, to make arrangements for their future together. However, when she got there she found that her lover had gone to Fife. When he came back he refused to meet her or to answer any of her letters. Broken hearted, Mary Cairns sought recompense in the courts. It would seem that Morris saw that the evidence against him was overwhelming and he agreed to settle. He paid her £50, and in addition the Sheriff ordered him to pay costs.

THE HEIGHT OF THE EMPIRE

A Long Way From Home
Source:
Glasgow Herald, Wednesday 25th June 1873
Otago Witness, Saturday 27th September 1873 (repeated in the West Coast Times, Tuesday 30th September 1873)
Clutha Leader, Friday 11th January 1878 and Friday 19th April 1878
Birmingham Post, Thursday 21st December 1876
Liverpool Mercury, Thursday 21st December 1876

Many Scots emigrated to Australia and New Zealand in the nineteenth century. In particular, they formed a strong community in the South Island of New Zealand. Newspaper evidence shows that there was not only an appetite amongst them to keep up with events in their native land but also the ability to do so, with stories often being reprinted. However, the accounts were often left a little vague as to dates, possibly to give the illusion that the reports were more current than they actually were. From 1876 onwards it became possible for information to be communicated much, much more quickly between Britain and the antipodes. Just 26 years after the laying of the first telegraph line across the English Channel, a cable was laid which linked London to New Zealand. However, one imagines that the activities of Linlithgowshire's criminal elements were low on the priority list for transmission down this technological miracle. A fine example of the sort of story that appeared, and the way it was related, comes from the pages of the Otago Witness, and was repeated word for word three days later in the West Coast Times (a paper published in the Canterbury area of New Zealand). The short article is worth repeating in full:

'The other day, at Linlithgow, a clerk was charged with stealing £81 from his employer. The jury found the charge not proven, and he was dismissed. An inspector of police, who was not satisfied of his innocence, watched him when he left the prison, and in a few hours he was caught taking the stolen money from a hiding-place in a field.'

Note: no source, no names and no dates!

In fact, the case had been reported in the Glasgow Herald three months earlier. The clerk in question was a Mr Monro, who worked for coal merchants, Messers John Watson & Sons. Monro had been tasked with taking £190 to the bank in Bathgate but had only deposited £109. The case was heard at the High Court of Justiciary in Edinburgh, and after being released, Monro took the train back to Bathgate, from where he travelled on to Armadale. All the while, he was being

The Height of the Empire

followed by a disguised Police Constable named Clark, following the orders of his Inspector. When the Constable saw Monro take the money from his hiding place, he began to chase him. Monro ran for it, dropping three of the £1 notes. This may have been an attempt to slow the policeman down, but if so it didn't work. He was caught with £78, and the three soggy notes were then recovered. Monro was taken to Bathgate Prison, and thence to Linlithgow where he was held pending further legal action.

So, the Otago Witness account seems to be inaccurate in a number of matters – the trial had been in Edinburgh, not Linlithgow, the policeman had been a constable, not an inspector, and he was working under orders, rather than following a hunch. However, it may not be the fault of the Witness – they mention a field, a detail not given in the Herald, so it may be that the story came to New Zealand from another source.

Two more examples come from another paper from the Otago area, the Clutha Leader, from the first half of 1878. Again, both articles are given in full. First, in January:

'A travelling blacksmith and his wife have been apprehended in Linlithgow for child-stealing. They were seen to abuse most cruelly a little girl of about eleven years, because she had not succeeded in begging sufficient for their rapacity, and on enquiry it was found that the poor thing had been stolen from Bristol by the pair.'

Then in April:

'Philip McArdel, 75 years of age, a vagrant, who died in a lodging-house in Linlithgow, left about £40 in one of his wallets, and £30 sewed between the lining and cloth of his coat. Besides these sums he also possessed two bottles full of sovereigns, both of which were hidden underground. A few hours before his death he made a will leaving his property equally between the lodging-house-keeper and the Rev. Mr McArtney, Roman Catholic priest, Linlithgow.'

Both stories clearly had a human interest element which makes the location largely irrelevant.

Another Linlithgowshire story from this period to be related outside Scotland was that of the butler (unnamed, of course, in the article) of Captain Robert Stewart of Westwood, which was covered in the Birmingham Post and Liverpool Mercury in 1876. The Captain took his man to court to accuse him of theft of some leftover

126 | Chapter Four

rabbit and bacon cutlets. The butler's conditions of employment were that he was to be paid through wages alone and that he was not to be provided with any food in the house. One morning, while clearing up after breakfast, he had succumbed to temptation and taken the cutlets. The court found that the butler was guilty, but that the case was so petty that no punishment was necessary other than a ticking off.

'A Disorderly Town Councillor'
Source:
The Scotsman, Wednesday 14th March 1877
Leeds Mercury, Friday 16th March 1877
Belfast News-Letter, Friday 23rd March 1877
Dundee Courier and Argus Northern Warder, Tuesday 27th March 1877 and Thursday 20th September 1877

Town councillors have not featured strongly in this book. One such illustrious figure, who found himself in the dock on at least two occasions in 1877, was Queensferry's Peter Pickard, a shoemaker by trade.

The first case was concerned with events on Tuesday 2nd March 1877. Despite there being four accounts, the sequence of events is a little unclear. The Dundee Courier seems to make most sense, though it shows what interest the case generated that it was reported in Leeds and Belfast, even if in a slightly garbled form.

The trial took place in the Linlithgow Sheriff Court. What seems to have happened is that on the evening of the day in question, Pickard and David Hill (a grocer, spirit dealer, one of the burgh magistrates and former Provost) gate-crashed a meeting of the Burgh Sanitary Committee, a body of which they were not members. They broke down the doors and Hill disrupted proceedings by taking all the chairs he could get his hands on, setting them up on the table and knocking them down, one after another. Several of the chairs were broken and the table was damaged. When the committee members took offence, he challenged one of them, Robert Anderson (a grocer) to a fight, then attacked him:

'with his fists and his coat'.

He then left the building and threw coppers to a large crowd of people who had gathered round. Meanwhile, Pickard was shouting that those present had no

The Height of the Empire

right to burn the town's gas, and ordering the burgh sanitary inspector, Thomas Hunter junior, to turn it off. When Hunter refused to comply, Pickard jumped onto the table and tried to turn it off himself. The committee members managed to get him off the table but he jumped back on and tried again. Being prevented yet again he tried to attack Hunter, and may or may not have punched him, depending whose account you believe.

Hill pled guilty and was fined £5 with the alternative of fourteen days imprisonment:

'the Sheriff remarking that as he (the accused) had often occasion to judge others, his behaviour was very unbecoming.'

Pickard actually had the temerity to plead not guilty. His counsel was Peter Miller of Linlithgow, who put forward the defence that, technically, the meeting had already been adjourned, and that it had not, in fact, been disturbed by Pickard's actions, which were a mere frolic. The judge didn't buy it and Pickard was found guilty of breach of the peace, though not of assault. He was fined £2, or fourteen days.

Six months later Pickard was back in the dock, this time at the Queensferry Sheriff Summary Court. The Dundee Courier related the trial of Pickard, John and George Black (both labourers) and Jane Pickard or Black. One may guess that John and George were Pickard's brothers-in-law.

Early on the morning of Sunday 2nd September, at between 2am and 3am (memories may have been a little hazy as to the exact time), the four of them were causing a disturbance in the street. It began with shouting and swearing, then some of those present stripped off some of their clothing and began fighting. In the struggle, they also assaulted and knocked down a telegraph clerk who just happened to be passing. The court found that the culprits were Pickard and John Black. Pickard was fined £1, or fourteen days imprisonment. Black got off a little more lightly with a fine of 15s or 10 days. The others were found not guilty.

THE HEIGHT OF THE EMPIRE

Infanticide
Source:
Aberdeen Weekly Journal, Tuesday 23rd October 1877

Today, the murder of a newborn child by its mother is seen as a double tragedy, likely to suggest that the woman is not in her right mind and in need of help. The summer of 1877 saw two cases of this type, which though in different parts of the country were understandably linked in the minds of the public, especially since both cases were heard in the High Court of Justiciary on 22nd October.

The first happened at Springfield Farm, on the outskirts of Linlithgow, on 24th June. In one of the fields, Margaret Crichton gave birth to a child which she strangled using hay. She pled guilty to culpable homicide, rather than murder, and was sentenced to five years of penal servitude.

On 2nd September, Maggie Mutch suffocated her newborn with a petticoat at a house near New Deer in Aberdeenshire. She then hid the body in a trunk. She too pled guilty to culpable homicide and was given the same sentence of five years penal servitude.

Both women were paupers, no husbands are mentioned, and Lord Deas, who heard the cases, commented that it was highly unsatisfactory that the Commissioners for the Poor had not considered the issues which these two cases highlighted to be worthy of investigation.

Complaints About the Court System
Source:
The Graphic, Saturday 17th November 1877

The Graphic was a weekly London paper that was printed between 1869 and 1932. In an article decrying the state of our courts Linlithgow got a small mention:

'Last week a Linlithgow jury having retired to consider their verdict sent the court-officer to tell the sheriff that no verdict would be given until refreshments had been supplied.'

The Height of the Empire

Impersonation and Theft
Source:
Glasgow Herald, Wednesday 29th January 1880
West Lothian Courier, Saturday 31st January 1880, Saturday 28th February, Saturday 24th April 1880, Saturday 29th May 1880 and Saturday 6th November 1880

Most of the crimes in this book demonstrated little in the way of subtlety or cunning and could be dealt with very quickly. We have seen that it was routine for multiple cases to be tried in one day. A slightly higher level of sophistication can be found in the case against William Walker and his wife Janet Walker, or Cunningham. This case lasted three days and saw over one hundred witnesses give evidence in Linlithgow Sheriff Court.

The story began on the evening of 6th October 1879 with a meeting of the Linlithgowshire Parish Funeral Society, in the Burgh Halls. This society was a major institution in the area, with 1,900 members, and no doubt held considerable funds. There must have been a financial element to the meeting, perhaps the collection of dues or paying out to the families of the deceased. In any case, when they had finished their business one of their number, Adam Deans, was instructed to carry the cash box back to the house of the treasurer, Archibald Lang.

The entrance to Lang's house was up a close, off the High Street. Approaching the foot of the steps up, Deans was met by Lang's daughter, Helen, in a state of agitation. Helen told him that her mother had taken ill very suddenly and asked him if he would be so good at to go and get a gill of whisky, presumably to help revive her, adding that she would take the cash box up. Mr Deans agreed to go on this errand and handed over the box, though he expressed concern that she might struggle with the weight. It was a sturdy item, and contained around £59, almost all of which was in silver. When he returned, he found Mrs Lang to be in fine health and no sign of Helen. She had been at the house that evening but had left much earlier with her brother and his wife. Deans went straight to the police and over the next few days extensive enquiries were undertaken.

Who was Helen's impersonator – someone who had managed to imitate her clothes, voice and manner? The police questioned people who had been in the locality that night and their investigations led them to search the home of William and Janet Walker. When they did so they found the substantial sum of £46 10s 3½d, nearly all in silver. William Walker was a failed publican, now working as a labourer and as such it seemed very unlikely that they would have that amount

130 | Chapter Four

of cash round the house. William could not account for it and Janet said that it was money which she had laid aside without her husband's knowledge while he was running his pub. This seemed at odds with the known money problems which the couple were having, with a number of creditors urgently demanding payment.

If events did unfold as Deans testified then the skill of the impersonation made it impossible to know who had perpetrated it. No one could positively tie the Walkers to the scene of the crime and the case against them was therefore circumstantial. Nevertheless, the Walkers were charged and brought to court. Many witnesses were called by both sides to try and show that Janet Walker was, or was not, in the vicinity at the time of the offence. Attempts were made to prove that the cash in question came from the box. Much was made of a burnt penny and a shilling with a hole through it which two Funeral Society men remembered being collected that evening. The defence council sought to prove that such coins were not as rare as the prosecution was trying to imply. Some people were found to speak extremely ill of Janet Walker's character, while others spoke in her favour. In the end the jury found that it could not lay the actual theft with sufficient certainty to the Walkers, yet they were satisfied that the money in their house was that which had been in the box taken from the Funeral Society. The result was that they found them both not guilty of theft (William, indeed, was cleared of all charges) but Janet was convicted of reset, or possession of stolen property. She was given a sentence of three months. If it really was her who carried out this impersonation then she was lucky to get such a short spell. If, however, she was innocent, she was robbed of her savings and three months of liberty.

The following month saw William Walker back in court, still protesting his wife's innocence and, under pressure from his creditors, arguing for the return of the money taken from their house. The Funeral Society was, of course, of the belief that it should be handed over to them. This might sound like an open and shut case, given the previous ruling, but it proved more complex. The proceedings dragged on through a number of hearings and come November 1880 the Funeral Society was asking its members for a contribution of 6d each to help in legal costs. This is the last mention of the case in the local newspaper so it may be that the Society failed to raise the money it needed and abandoned the cause.

The Height of the Empire

The Case That Never Was
- 'The Right of Fishing in Linlithgow Loch'

Part 1 - A Call to Action
Source:
Glasgow Herald, Wednesday 26th March 1879

In the 1840s Linlithgow had found itself with severely scorched fingers when it took on the Edinburgh and Glasgow Railway over customs duties. Memories of the years of costly legal hearing were no doubt not far from the surface when the great fishing rights dispute arose in 1879. Like the tolls which the town had enjoyed for centuries until beaten by the railway company, fishing on the Loch was something that had always been accepted as one of the privileges of the residents. The Crown, however, believed that it owned the Loch as well as the Palace and the Peel. When the Crown served notice that it intended to take its ownership of the Loch seriously, and would go through the Court of Session to do so, there was outrage in the town.

A public meeting was held in the Town Hall on the evening of Monday 24th March. It was called by the Provost to discuss whether or not the townspeople wished to contend the action. Provost Dawson opened the meeting, addressing it at considerable length. It seemed that the representatives of the Crown had felt provoked to assert their rights following the catching of eels in the Loch during the recent severe frost. The Crown claimed ownership of the Loch and the solum and had announced that it intended to produce a plan showing where the boundaries lay. The reporter recorded Provost Dawson's questions about the conditions under which this would be decided:

'Was it to be when the Loch was in its present condition – choking up the town's drains, flooding the houses, and rendering the west end scarcely habitable? Or was it to be in the middle of summer, or at the time when the Loch was so low that the Provost's father ploughed it at the east end?'

The Crown was maintaining that the townspeople did not have, and had never had, any right to use the Loch or its contents. What, asked Provost Dawson, were the town's tanners to do? The tanners washed their hides in the Loch. What about people who drew off water to wash their clothes? If the Crown got all it was looking for, he went on:

The Height Of The Empire

'the people would hardly be allowed to look at the Loch at all.'

He invited the meeting to support the Council in contesting the case. Mr Mickel proposed a motion to that effect, seconded by Mr Beattie.

Councillor McAlpine mounted the platform. He argued that with the passing of the Parks Act[8] some years previously, which the Council had supported, they had no leg to stand on, and that even if the case was won in the Court of Session, the Crown would appeal, taking it to the House of Lords. He asked if those present were prepared to take the case that far, with little chance of success? He felt that the key entitlement which the town needed was to be able to run the drains into the Loch and proposed an amendment that this be the only matter on which action was taken. He was not able to find a seconder.

George Dougal felt that there remained time to enter into discussions with the Crown. He proposed that a committee be formed to ascertain what they really meant, and to report back to a public meeting. This was seconded by Joseph Mackie, Sheriff-Clerk. Mr Mickel and Mr Beattie withdrew their motion in favour of Mr Dougal's, which was adopted by the meeting. Five men were appointed to the committee: George Dougal (shoe manufacturer), Peter Miller (solicitor), Mr Mackie, James Law (inspector of poor) and George Waldie (printer).

Part 2 - A Dash of Reality
Source:
Glasgow Herald, Monday 14th April 1879

On Friday 11th May, just over two weeks later, a second public meeting was held in the Town Hall, called *'by tuck of drum'*. The hall was well filled, and so was the platform: as well as the five men appointed at the previous meeting, it contained, Provost Dawson, Bailies Dougal and Hardie, Commissioners Jamieson, Hutton, Meek, and McAlpine and Mr Aitken, clerk to the Police Commission.

The meeting opened with a summary of the previous meeting and an update on what had happened since. An eminent Edinburgh lawyer, Mr Wotherspoon, had been engaged, while Robert Aitken had been appointed as the local agent, responsible for briefing Mr Wotherspoon. Initially, Wotherspoon advised them that a lot of preparation needed to be done before they could take the case to court, and that the proximity of the Easter holidays was going to hold things up. Mr Wotherspoon had met with a lawyer representing the Crown and shortly afterwards resigned his appointment as hopeless.

The Height of the Empire

The near unanimity of the previous meeting appears to have been shattered. The town was unable to present a united front. The Provost told the meeting that some lochside proprietors:

'like Hal o' the Wynd, would only fight for their own.'

Councillor McAlpine's view of the case from the previous meeting seemed to have gained currency: there was a feeling that the only issue worth fighting on was the drains, and it was unclear if the Crown had any intention of preventing this. Against that, the meeting was reminded that two years previously the town had been warned under the Public Health Act that the Loch was becoming *'prejudicial to the health of the inhabitants,'* and that Forfar had been compelled, under similar circumstances, to create a proper sewerage system at great expense.

Fears were raised, again, about whether or not a case could be won, and the cost of undertaking it. When a motion was put to the vote calling for the Council to pursue legal action only one hand was raised in favour. The town had surrendered.

Part 3 - A New Flashpoint
Source:
Glasgow Herald, Wednesday 13th July 1881
West Lothian Courier, Saturday 16th July 1881

The story, however, does not end at that point. Two years on, in 1881, the Board of Works had leased the fishing rights for the Loch to an Edinburgh fishmonger, Mr Jamieson. He objected to locals fishing with rod and line from the loch bank and complained to the Board and they ordered their man on the spot, the palace ranger, to patrol the area and stop them. The West Lothian Courier describes how:

'on a summer evening scores of working men may be seen at the back of the Loch enjoying themselves.'

This caused much local indignation; articles were written using the phrase *'from time immemorial'* and the cry went up for something to be done. In response to the considerable discontent, a special meeting of the Town Council was called for Monday 11th July by Provost Mackie. The townspeople decided to meet at the Town Hall at 8pm, to hear the outcome, and the town's drummer, Tom Heugh, was sent round to make the populace aware.

In the Council meeting, it was accepted that the Crown had the right to control fishing. However, it was believed that Mr Jamieson himself had said that his interest lay only in the eels, and that the few perch and roach which were being caught were therefore of no consequence to him. The Council decided that the Board of Works should be petitioned to take a lenient approach, with a copy of their letter to be sent to the local MP, Mr Ramsay.

Following the Council meeting, Provost Mackie went into session with the Commissioners of Police, perhaps to discuss how men caught fishing by the ranger should be dealt with. A crowded meeting waited patiently for the Council to appear before them:

'an occasional ruff and exclamation from Tom Heugh being all that occurred to diversify the monotony'.

At 9pm the Provost and other members of the Council entered the hall to loud cheering. Provost Mackie spoke in a conciliatory way. He said that while he had not been responsible for the calling of the meeting he could understand why the inhabitants had taken it upon themselves. He told them the decision of the Council, to petition the Board and involve the MP. He explained that the Crown was within its rights, but that they hoped that an accommodation could be made. He urged patience and told those assembled:

'In the meantime do not give the Crown, or the Crown's tenant, any hold over any single inhabitant of Linlithgow; obey the law, like good citizens as you are, and by this petition and by the action of our member get the law altered.'

The meeting voted to leave the matter in the hands of the Council and ended with a vote of thanks to the Provost.

Part 4 - Peaceful Co-existence
Source:
Glasgow Herald, Friday 21st March 1884, Wednesday 16th April 1884, Tuesday 27th May 1884, Monday 27th December 1886 and Monday 31st August 1891

It is unclear exactly how events developed but by 1884 peace had been established. The previous year another Edinburgh fishmonger, Mr Anderson, had taken up the lease with a view to establishing a trout hatchery. By February

The Height of the Empire

1884 he had released 300,000 ova, which shows the scale of the operation, then in April of that year, it was noted that the Town Council were discussing proposals to make improvements to the drains into the Loch. This would suggest that the main fear of the townspeople had not come to pass. In May, Mr Anderson held a grand opening ceremony with a select group of invited guests. Having been shown round his new buildings and equipment, the VIPs were rowed from the nets in the north east of the Loch to the south east, and:

'proceeded to the Star and Garter, where a capital luncheon was provided'.

In the chair was none other than Provost Mackie, who led toasts to the success of the hatchery. Interestingly, one of the other toasts was to the continued suitability of the Loch for angling (though no doubt in a controlled manner). It may have been that the new trout hatchery had resulted in the creation of jobs for some local people, and changing attitudes both at the Council and amongst the populace.

Two years later there are accounts of a curling match on the Loch on Christmas Day and then in 1891 a rowing regatta was reported. The crown and the burgh seem to have found the means to share the amenities of the Loch without further conflict.

Chapter Five
1881-1900 – The end of the Century

The End Of The Century

Introduction

The last two decades of the nineteenth century saw the British economy stuttering along as it sought to find a way out of the Long Depression, finally emerging in 1896. The British Empire continued to expand, especially in Africa, and by the mid '90s one person in four across the world was a subject of Queen Victoria.

Britain was no longer unmatched in the economic sphere, having been caught by the United States and rivalled by an even newer country, Germany.

During the course of the century the economy of Linlithgow had changed dramatically. The trades which had dominated the burgh for centuries were largely disbanded, or reduced to a ceremonial role. Shoemaking alone remained strong. The Ordnance Gazetteer of Scotland (published in 1884) describes the principal industries, in addition to shoemaking, as *'two paper-mills, two distilleries, a soap works, and sawmills'.* In the south of the county, shale was king. The Gazetteer also gives us an idea of the types of social activities that ordinary people could take part in. In Linlithgow itself the author noted a bowling club, a bicycle club, a curling club, a company of volunteers (riflemen), a horticultural society, a mechanics' institute, a workingmen's club and a workingmen's hall.

This period saw the beginning of a further transport revolution. In the first two decades of the century travel across the country had been by foot, horse or carriage on very poor roads. The 1820s had seen the construction of hundreds of miles of canals. The 1840s onwards had seen the canals eclipsed by the railways. A story from Monday 4th May 1896 in the Glasgow Herald shows that the picture was about to change again. The opening sentences read:

'It is claimed on behalf of horseless carriages that they can be run at any rate of speed up to twenty miles an hour; that they can be manipulated more easily than a horse and carriage; that they can be taken up an incline of 1 in 8 and turned in a twelve-feet circle; that they can be driven by a non-technical man; and that the cost of running is less that 1/2d per mile. If only one-half of all this is true, there can be no doubt that the future of such vehicles is secure, and that the building of them will in time develop into an enormous industry.'

How right the author was. The changes in transport show, as well as any other example, the huge technological progress that had been made in the course of one hundred years. Britain, and indeed Linlithgowshire in 1900 was a very

THE END OF THE CENTURY

different place from 1800.

The penal system had also seen many changes, though in some ways the debate had come full circle. In their report of 1895, the Gladstone Committee spoke positively about the benefits which had been delivered through the centralisation of the prison service and the implementation of uniform standards. However, in words which harked back to early reformers such as Elizabeth Fry and Jeremy Bentham, they stated that, *'We start from the principle that prison treatment should have as its priority and concurrent objects, deterrence and reformation.'* They believed that the effect of a spell in prison on the inmates should be *'to turn them out of prison better men and women physically and morally than when they came in.'* The treadmill and the crank were out, and books and educational opportunities were in. For the first time, thought was given to how to prevent prisoners reoffending on their release: they recommended partnership working between the prison service and voluntary organisations to manage the reintegration of prisoners into society. Their report formed the basis of the 1898 Prison Act, and was seen as the definitive work on the subject for 50 years.

Murder: Alleged and Attempted
Source:
Aberdeen Weekly Journal, Tuesday 6th November 1883
The Scotsman, Wednesday 7th November 1883
Aberdeen Weekly Journal, Wednesday26th December 1883
Glasgow Herald, Tuesday 24 August 1886

Two cases of domestic violence in Linlithgowshire made the newspapers again at the end of 1883. The first involved a Bo'ness man called Francis Kane, or Cain, and came before the High Court of Justiciary in Edinburgh in early November. The second must have caused a sensation, involving as it did a highly respected man in Bo'ness and Linlithgow. The third case in this section occurred three years later and involved the death of a Bo'ness man at the hands of his neighbours.

Part 1 - Francis Kane and the death of Mary Creely
To deal first with Kane first, he was charged with murdering his wife, Mary Creely, at their home in Furnace Rows (near Bo'ness) on the 12th or 13th of July. That she was dead, there was no doubt, and it was alleged that he had:

'struck her repeatedly on the face and head, knocked her to the floor, kicked her in the

The End Of The Century

head and abdomen and violently trampled on her'.

Cain pled not guilty to murder and once again the trial seems to have hinged on his intent. As in the cases of the two Uphall wife killers in the previous chapter, it seems that there was a tendency for juries to give men the benefit of the doubt when wife beating resulted in death. After the evidence had been heard, including the words of the dying woman, the jury found him guilty of the reduced charge of culpable homicide. The Scotsman recorded the words of the judge, Lord Young, to Kane:

'Francis Kane, I have considered the sentence which it is my duty to pronounce upon you in consequence of the verdict now read. The verdict convicts you of having killed your wife, not in circumstances amounting to murder, but to have culpably killed her, and it certainly appears that you killed her with considerable violence, although probably, no doubt, you thought that when your wife said that you danced upon her that was exaggerated language, because if it had been the nature of the case, you would probably have been convicted of another crime. Exaggerated language from her was perhaps not wonderful, considering the account we have had of her habits and her mode of speaking, but undoubtedly you somehow produced a rupture by considerable violence, which terminated the existence of the mother of your children, and your companion of upwards of forty years. Your own feelings, if you have the feelings of a man at all, must constitute the chief part of your punishment. The jury, looking to the whole circumstances that there was no premeditation, and that in a state of partial intoxication at least – probably on both sides – you were roused by her conduct to use that violence, which no doubt you did not intend, to deprive her of life, or to do her any serious injury, the jury have recommended you to mercy. Nevertheless, the fact remains that you have killed your wife by violence, and it is impossible to visit that with anything but a severe sentence. I must sentence you, old as you are, for that crime, to penal servitude, but I limit it – having regarded the nature of the verdict, the recommendation of the jury, and your age – to a period of five years.'

Part 2 – A Most Respectable Man

A month later the people of the county were no doubt shocked to hear of the *'cowardly and cruel'* behaviour, to paraphrase the Sheriff, of Samuel Gibson, a successful man who had chemist shops in Bo'ness and Linlithgow.

He was accused of assaulting his wife, Mary, and mother-in-law, in their house in Linlithgow High Street on a number of occasions between 17th November and 11th December. Things had come to a head on the morning of the latter date, as

Mary Gibson told the court. The bulk of the newspaper article was based on her testimony.

On the morning of the 11th, after at least a month of verbal and possibly physical abuse, Mary and Samuel had been quarrelling yet again. Finally, Mary had had enough and told her husband that she was going to go to the Sheriff to seek a legal separation from him. Samuel told her she should go, and as she was trying to leave he punched her on the cheek. Mary got out of the house, and stayed out until eight that night. When she got back, she found her husband there, and intent on picking up the quarrel where they had left off. He told their servant girl to go out as he had a job to do that night and wanted no witnesses. This chilling revelation caused a sensation in the court!

As soon as the girl had left he locked the door then ran at Mary, putting his hands round her throat, and, apparently, striking her on the head (which would appear to need extraordinary dexterity, if not an extra arm). He told her that she would be dead that night and he the next day (more sensation in the court)! He said that he was going to kill her mother and that he would rather be hanged than carry on living like this. Mary told how she escaped from his clutches and ran to another room where a sick boy was lying. Gibson then armed himself with the kitchen poker and came after her. He grabbed her and was dragging her into the kitchen when they heard a knock on the door. It was Mr Rae (presumably a neighbour), who called on Gibson to open up. Gibson let go of his wife and told her that he was going to get his pistol. He said that if Rae came in *'he would not go out a living man'* (yet more sensation!). Just then, the police broke down the door and he was arrested.

A number of witnesses, including Mary's mother and Rae's wife, Elizabeth, are reported to have corroborated her evidence. Strangely, there is no mention of Mr Rae testifying, or the mysterious sick boy, though he may have been too young.

Gibson's guilt was clear to the court. Considering that he could have been construed to have been attempting to murder his wife he could perhaps have felt himself lucky to escape with a sentence of 60 days imprisonment.

Part 3 – The Death of Walter Russell
In previous chapters we have seen men hung or transported for long periods of time for causing the death of one of their fellow humans. A case from 1886 shows a much more lenient approach being taken.

The End Of The Century

On 23rd August 1886 William Murray and Alexander Barras were brought from prison in Edinburgh to stand before Sheriff Crichton at the Sheriff Court in Linlithgow. The two men were miners and lived in Kinneil Rows, near Bo'ness. They were charged with attacking and assaulting with their fists Walter Russell, another miner, who lived in Snab Rows, also near Bo'ness.

The attack had taken place on the morning of Sunday 4th July and had been so severe that Russell had died shortly afterwards from his injuries. The first piece of good news for the accused was that they were found guilty of culpable homicide rather than murder. This charge could still lead to a heavy sentence so it seems rather surprising that they received only six months imprisonment each.

Frauds and Slanders
Source:
Aberdeen Weekly Journal, Saturday 8th December 1883 and Thursday 13th May 1886
Glasgow Herald, Thursday 13th May 1886 and Thursday 8th July 1886
The Scotsman, Friday 19th November 1886

If at first you don't succeed, try, try again, the saying goes. George Thomson, a cattle dealer from the Falkirk area, certainly kept trying, and the result was that he kept getting tried.

On Wednesday 5th December 1883 he found himself appearing before Sheriff Blair at Inverness Sheriff Court. Thomson had attended a cattle market in Muir of Ord in October, something which in itself demonstrates a degree of mobility which would have been remarkable in the first half of the century. At the market, he bought cows from three northern farmers, and paid each of them by cheque. Unfortunately, each of these cheques bounced, Thomson's bank account being empty. Clearly cheques had been causing some difficulties across the country for only the preceding year the government had passed the Bills of Exchange Act to properly define and regulate them. Now, it would seem that either Thomson had not got the hang of this form of payment, or was stupid or desperate, because it emerged in court that this was far from the first time that he had run into this difficulty. In fact, the court was told that he was already awaiting trial on similar charges in Linlithgow, Falkirk and Lanark!

Sadly, this does not seem to have been an isolated incident. One can imagine that cattle dealers from the Falkirk/Linlithgow area might be getting a bad reputation. In May 1886 the Aberdeen Weekly Journal reported an action brought by William Alexander, a cattle dealer from Whitburn, against Peter Byers, a farmer and cattle dealer from the West Calder area. Alexander was suing Byers for the enormous sum of £5,000 for slander.

Alexander stated that on 16th July 1884 he had given Byers two cheques for a total of £650, as well as £170 in cash by way of a short term loan. All seemed to be proceeding normally until Byers discovered that a bank order had been presented, written on a half sheet of notepaper, which stated:

'West Calder, July 21. 1884. – The Commercial Bank of Scotland, Limited; pay to William Alexander, or bearer, the sum of £900 sterling. Peter Byers.'

According to Alexander, Byers presented him with this bank order by way of repayment for the loan. According to Byers, he never wrote any such document and Alexander forged it. Byers complained to the authorities and nearly a year later, on 12th June 1885, the case came before Linlithgow Sheriff Court. Byers stated that his signature had been forged and as a result, Alexander was arrested and held for nearly a month, until 7th July.

Alexander was not happy: he came out of prison protesting his innocence, claiming that he had been slandered by Byers and wrongfully imprisoned as a result. The following July the parties found themselves in the Court of Session. We know many trials to have been very short, making the five days the Court spent investigating this case noteworthy, especially since there cannot have been a huge amount of evidence.

Byers maintained his stance that the signature on the bill was not his, and there seems to have been no dispute at this stage that it was indeed a forgery. On the other side, no-one seemed to be trying to prove that Alexander had been responsible for said forgery. The key point of debate seems to have been whether or not Byers' words or actions had led to Alexander being wrongfully detained. Though there were suggestions that Byers had made allegations against Alexander in private, the prosecution was unable to prove it conclusively, and he had never said as much in a court of law. The jury, unanimously, found in favour of Byers. Alexander wasn't finished yet and in November 1886 he petitioned for a retrial: the courts were having none of it.

The End Of The Century

'An Elopement and its Consequences'
Source:
Aberdeen Weekly Journal, Friday 26th December 1890 and Monday 29th December 1890

Nineteenth century Britain was a land where far fewer people owned their own homes than today. Many people helped to make ends meet through taking in lodgers. Sometimes this had unfortunate consequences.

Once again, Linlithgow Sheriff Court was the setting in which the events were laid out. It was Sheriff Dougal's duty to examine a miner called Peter Devine. He had been lodging for some time with fellow miner James Harkin and his wife in Blackburn. Harkin told the court how over a number of months:

'an intimacy sprang up between the accused and Mrs Harkin.'

Harkin told the court that on several occasions he had gone into his house and found his wife and Devine engaged in earnest conversation, which they had quickly broken off.

The previous Sunday, Harkin and Devine had both been scheduled for the night shift. Harkin had gone to work as usual but Devine had said that he was feeling sick and had stayed at home. When Harkin came back from work the next morning he was *'surprised'* to find the house locked up and his wife and Devine gone. Not only that, but Devine had taken some of the injured man's clothes with him!

Harkin contacted the police who quickly traced the runaways to the village of Crossgates in Fife. Devine was arrested and charged with theft (of the clothes, not the wife). In court, Mrs Harkin said that she had never been happy in her marriage, and had been in such a hurry to get away that she hadn't given much thought to what they were taking with them. The Sheriff admonished her, telling her that a wife was not entitled to take away articles which did not belong to her when leaving her husband. Devine's guilt seems to have been beyond doubt – after all, he was found with the clothes. However, in a curious ruling, the Sheriff found him guilty but let him go free. It would seem that he was, in effect, sentenced to the days he had already spent in custody.

THE END OF THE CENTURY

Bible Bashers
Source:
Aberdeen Weekly Journal, Tuesday 24th February 1891

The Salvation Army was founded in 1865 and was spreading across Scotland by the 1880s. In 1891, a number of the members of the Uphall Tabernacle found themselves in Linlithgow Sheriff Court following some ungodly behaviour. At the end of a meeting on 7th February, David Nicolson got into a furious argument with another member, John Brown, about a biblical matter. The events are not entirely clear, but it would seem that Nicolson wouldn't let the matter lie, while others were trying to shut up the hall for the night. Brown was told to put off the gas lights, which irritated Nicolson so much that he struck him. Captain Lucy Heltzer became embroiled and was also assaulted! The Sheriff bound Nicolson over to keep the peace.

Birds of a Feather
Source:
Newcastle Weekly Courant, Saturday 30th April 1892

The courts retained corporal punishment as a weapon in the fight against relatively minor crime. Indeed, for juvenile crime, sheriffs had the power to order up to 36 strokes of the birch or tawse until 1948. For adults, it was rarely used in Scotland by the nineteenth century and had effectively been abolished in 1862.

Sixteen year old Hugh Meechan and his friend, Henry Bryce, were found guilty at Linlithgow Sheriff Court of pulling feathers out of a peacock's tail. Sixteen was the upper age for juveniles in the eyes of the law in Scotland. Perhaps Meechan was seen as the more serious offender as he was sentenced to a week in prison. Bryce received six stripes with a birch rod.

Child Abuse
Source:
Aberdeen Weekly Journal, Wednesday 4th February 1891 and Thursday 19th May 1892
Glasgow Herald, Wednesday 25th August 1897

Two Linlithgowshire cases of cruelty by parents to their children are brought together here, both reported in the Aberdeen Weekly Journal in the early

The End Of The Century

1890s. A further story from five years later which has similarities, but important differences, is also included in this section.

Part 1 – 'Alleged Inhumanity to Children By a Mother'

This first, from 1891, was a most distressing case from the Linlithgow Sheriff Court. A Bo'ness widow called Isabella Scotland was examined by the Sheriff as a result of which she was brought to trial to face a number of charges of child cruelty. It was alleged that over a nine month period she had barbarously assaulted five of her children. The children in question were aged between six months and twelve years old and the court heard that she had beaten them with heavy weapons, kicked them and kept them inadequately dressed. Witnesses reported that the children were constantly dirty and overrun with vermin. Not surprisingly, medical examination had found them to have many cuts and bruises.

The Sheriff ruled that Scotland be committed to prison until further investigations could be held.

Part 2 – 'Shocking Cruelty'

The same newspaper reported another incident the following May. Again, the case was heard at Linlithgow Sheriff Court by Sheriff Melville. James Malley, a miner from East Benhar, near Whitburn, was charged with:

'having cruelly ill-treated and neglected his child Alexander, aged four years, by failing to provide him with food sufficient and proper for his nourishment, and by abusing him repeatedly with a poker and a whip.'

The authorities were alerted to the abuse by some of Malley's neighbours, who had been so concerned that they had contacted the police. The court heard that the boy was kept barefoot right through the winter and at times he looked for refuge at the houses of the neighbours. One woman testified that on one particular night she had gone into the house and found the boy lying underneath the bed with his head resting on a piece of coal.

Though he protested his innocence, Malley was found guilty. Sentencing him to two months hard labour, the Sheriff described his treatment of his son as brutal and horrible.

In the same vein, the same edition recorded a case which happened in Manchester. Eliza Armstrong, a married woman, was accused of murdering her

The End Of The Century

child by drowning it in a wash-tub. Questioned, Armstrong told the court that something had caused her to do it, and she could not help it. The jury concluded that she had not been responsible for her actions and the judge ruled that she be detained indefinitely.

Part 3 - 'Cruelty to Children'
A few years later, the Glasgow Herald reported another case of child neglect from Linlithgowshire, but with a slight twist to it.
Broxburn labourer John Woods was charged with neglecting his five children. The prosecution described them as being:

'in a fearful state with dirt and vermin, so much so that a doctor had to be called in to examine one of the children.'

Woods told the court that his wife was no longer living with him and that he was doing the best he could. He called one of his daughters as a witness and got her to testify that she and her siblings were well fed and attended to. Other testimony, however, contradicted this, which, combined with the police and medical evidence led him to be found guilty. However, given his marital circumstances, the Sheriff let him off with an admonishment.

The Evils of Alcohol
Source:
Newcastle Weekly Courant, Saturday 11th June 1892
Aberdeen Weekly Journal, Saturday 28th January 1893 and Thursday 4th January 1894
Glasgow Herald, Saturday 4th January 1896

As in all decades, drink lay behind many crimes and unfortunate incidents.

The General News column in the 11th June 1892 edition of the Newcastle Weekly Courant carried two stories relating to alcohol. In Linlithgow, shoemaker William Watt pled guilty to the charge that on 27th May he had stolen a bottle of whisky from a drunk man near St Magdalen's. He was sentenced to one month in prison.

The second story occurred near Skipton. On the preceding Monday night Thomas Brackenbury, described as 'a tramping twister', and Joseph Cook had been drinking heavily together. They:

The End Of The Century

'adjourned together to the canal bank to wrestle for another pint of beer.'

Unfortunately, they both rolled into the canal and Brackenbury drowned.

Drink seems to have had a major part to play in a story from the Aberdeen Weekly Journal from the following year, regarding a case heard at Linlithgow Sheriff Court. On 10th June 1893, Allan Nicol, a labourer, resident in Kirk's Close, Bo'ness, came before Sheriff Melville charged with stabbing his wife on 18th May. The two had been drunk and had fallen into a row about money matters. Nicol had attacked his wife with a tobacco knife and wounded her on the right eyebrow. The wound is described as being a severe one. The Sheriff found Nicol guilty. The journalist recorded Melville's comments:

'He said no doubt the prisoner did not know very well what he was doing, and in his drunken state, and with what mind he had, which was not very much, he had stabbed his wife.'

Melville imposed the upper limit of the sentence available to him, which was a jail term of sixty days.

The next story comes from 1894. Given the problems which the demon drink could cause, Alexander Mather, a publican from Grangepans, might have argued that he was doing a public service when he was found by Sheriff Melville to have watered down his whisky by 30%. Instead he took a line of defence which was equally unlikely to succeed – he argued that the whisky was of good quality and too strong to sell in its original form: his mistake was to have erroneously watered it down too much. He was fined £2. Bad as this crime was, it was not considered to be as serious as that committed by dairyman George Gardner. He was found guilty of selling low fat milk! He had surreptitiously removed 20% of the cream, for which he was fined 3 guineas.

More dramatic was the final story in this section, dating to 1896, which brought together that classic combination – alcohol and domestic violence. It has a nice turn of phrase and reads in full:

'MORE WIFE-BEATING AT IRVINE – At a Burgh Police Court yesterday – Baillie Miller on the bench – John Green, from Peter Street, was convicted on evidence of having assaulted his wife on Thursday night. The husband's wrath had been roused because his wife refused to drink whisky from a bottle brought into the house. The police found the woman's face swollen and bleeding. Green complained that his wife

was always running for the police; and the fiscal observed to the Court that there was evidently good cause. The police experienced great difficulty in getting Green conveyed to the lock-up. He was fined 30s, or in default 30 days' imprisonment.'

One wonders if either, or both, of the stories in the next section could also have been included in this one as they may well have been alcohol related – of course, the same argument could also be made for many of the cases of violence in this book.

Assaulting a Police Officer
Source:
Glasgow Herald, Monday 3rd December 1883
Glasgow Herald, Saturday 29th September 1894

This pair of stories, involving assaults on policemen, are separated by just over a decade. The second sounds like a more serious case for two reasons. Firstly, the offender had committed more than one assault, and secondly, he had assaulted a more senior officer.

The earlier case, dating from the start of December 1883, saw the trial of James Black, a labourer, before Sheriff Melville at Linlithgow Sheriff Court. Black was found guilty of assaulting a police constable in Kirkliston on 6th November and sentenced to 60 days hard labour.

The second case occurred in 1894, and saw James Stevenson, a miner, appear before Linlithgow Sheriff Court to face multiple counts of assault. Firstly, it was alleged that he had fallen out with John Anderson, a fellow miner, and attacked him with a pick handle in an attempt to prevent him from going to work! On the second occasion, which had occurred on the 26th September, he had assaulted Robert Chalmers, Inspector of Police, in Armadale. Presumably there being no pick handle (or other weapon) to hand, he had improvised:

'beating him with his head and attempting to bite him.'

Stevenson was freed on the payment of £15 bail.

The End Of The Century

Health and Safety
Source:
Glasgow Herald, Monday 20th March 1893, Saturday 12th June 1897 and Tuesday 3rd May 1898
Aberdeen Weekly Journal, Wednesday 20th September 1899

We tend to think of the Victorian age as a time when people endured harsh working conditions and gave little, if any, thought to health and safety, and over the course of this book we have seen how these concepts began to make legal progress. In March 1893 the Glasgow Herald reported a case where one of the county's many oil companies was taken to task, and a case from 1897 shows how risky working life remained on the railways. Two cases from 1898 and 1899 shed light on the dangers of mining. All these cases were heard in Linlithgow Sheriff Court.

Going back to 1893, John Hamilton, a miner from Mossend, West Calder, sued the Hermand Oil Company, also of West Calder, for £100, following the death of his four year old son, William, a year before. The poor boy's head had been crushed by pumping equipment at Hermand's No. 1 pit, at Breich Works. Sheriff Melville's conclusions were reported as follows:

'The defenders were bound to foresee such a likely occurrence as that which befell the child, and to provide against it. They might have done so by fencing the shafting so as to prevent the child going near the pit. If the gate at the opening of the shaft had been in position the boy could not have his head in danger. But the engineman had removed the gate, and the defenders were responsible for the act.'

He awarded Hamilton the full £100 of his claim. It is interesting to note that though just a poor man, Hamilton's case was put by a solicitor, Mr James F. MacDonald.

We haven't had a murder yet in this chapter, and we aren't going to, though we have seen quite a number of men convicted of culpable homicide following overly energetic assaults. The case against John Graham was also for culpable homicide, but for very different reasons.

Graham was a foreman blacksmith who worked for the North British Railway Company at Falkirk. He was charged with causing the death of a Falkirk engineer called Colin Muir and appeared before Linlithgow Sheriff Court on Friday 11 June 1897.

Chapter Five

The End Of The Century

Graham and Muir were two of a number of men working on the construction of a new bridge on a branch line which ran between Bathgate Lower Station and Bathgate Upper Station on 1st June. The work involved the use of a portable crane, which had been placed on top of a wagon. However, on the day in question it hadn't been properly secured, for which Graham was held responsible. As a result, when it was being used to lift some pieces of track, it toppled over. Colin Muir was trapped between the crane and a signal box on the embankment and crushed so badly that he died within an hour. Another workman, called Cochrane, was also seriously injured, but was recovering. Graham was freed on the payment of £5 bail.

Mines could be dangerous places for a number of reasons. Combustible gases caused explosions in many pits across the country: in 1898 alone there were explosions in Coatbridge, Ayr and Bo'ness, amongst others. The Bo'ness explosion resulted in the introduction of increased safety procedures which saw George Burden and Robert Rooney taken to court for contravention of the Coal Mines Regulation Act.

One of the new measures was to search the men to ensure that no hazardous items were taken below ground. During a search at Snab Pit, Burden, from Furnace Rows, Bo'ness, had been found to have several lucifers (matches) in his possession. Burden pled guilty but by way of explanation told the court that it had been, until recently, the custom for men to carry naked lights in the pit. Matches were now banned, lit or not, and Burden said that he had simply forgotten that day that he had some in his pocket – and that he had no intention of using them in violation of the regulations. The Sheriff-Substitute decided to accept his explanation and gave him a minimal fine of 5s, or three days imprisonment.

On the same day, in the same court, Robert Rooney was accused of smoking at the Furnace Yard Pit in Bo'ness, a pit which had recently suffered an explosion which killed three men. He denied the charge, but admitted smoking *'in what is known as the haulage road'* where it was not prohibited. He was given the same punishment as Burden.

A case the following year (1899) illustrated that mine owners were being forced to take the safety of their workers seriously, or pay (literally) the consequences. Mrs Sarah Macaulay (nee Bonar) had lost her husband, Dennis, in a mining accident in Uphall in 1898. The court awarded her £234 under the Workmen's Compensation Act, but with strings attached. The Sheriff gave instructions that

Chapter Five | 151

The End Of The Century

£156, or two thirds of the money, was to be invested in the Post Office Savings Bank on behalf of the Macaulay's daughter, Jane.

'Soldiers Charged with Theft'
Source:
Glasgow Herald, Thursday 10th October 1895

Though we may think of Blackness Castle as belonging to the mediaeval period it was used by the British Army into the early years of the twentieth century. In fact, the castle saw a considerable amount of construction work during the nineteenth century, most of which was stripped out in the late 1920s and early 1930s as part of a programme of restoration works.

From 1870 to 1912 it was a major ammunition depot. It was during this phase that Privates William Horsburgh and John McNaught of the Black Watch found themselves in Linlithgow Sheriff Court, escorted by an unnamed lieutenant.

On the day of their misbehaviour, the two soldiers had been granted passes by the commanding officer until midnight. They admitted that as the evening wore on they became the worse for liquor. They ended the night's entertainment by going into a garden in the nearby village and helping themselves to apples. They pled guilty to the charges brought against them for their actions and the Sheriff decided to let them off with an admonishment. However, it seems that this was more than a one-off occurrence as the court heard that a number of incidents of stealing had been reported to the local police, and it was suspected that soldiers from the garrison were to blame. The Sheriff observed that the commanding officer should:

'consider whether the existing arrangements for granting passes should be continued.'

The lieutenant promised to convey the suggestion to the colonel. Very good of him!

Poaching – Still a Serious Matter
Source:
Glasgow Herald, Saturday 5th September 1896, Saturday 4th January 1896 and

The End Of The Century

Thursday 19th July 1900

During the course of this book we have seen poaching cases reported throughout the whole length of the nineteenth century, and it is clear that as an issue for landowners, it remained significant right through the period. Two cases from Linlithgow Sheriff Court from 1896 give a flavour of how such cases were dealt with at the close of the century, and of the complications which could arise in establishing the facts. We will look first at a case from September 1896, which was given more detailed treatment in the press, then at the case from the start of that year. A third case follows from 1900, which illustrates a further variation.

The September 1896 case appeared under the headline *'AN EXTRAORDINARY POACHING PROSECUTION'.* It gives interesting insights into the working of the court on cases like this. What made the case extraordinary was the way in which one of the witnesses behaved rather than the crime itself.

The accused were two miners called David Johnston and Francis Croft. On 2nd September they were stopped by a police constable coming from lands near Bathgate. The policeman suspected that they had been poaching and searched them, finding fourteen rabbits in their possession!

In court, Johnston and Croft did not dispute that they had had the rabbits but denied poaching. Johnston claimed that he had permission from the shooting tenants[9] of two of the farms in the area to kill rabbits and hares, and that it was from one of these farms that he had got the animals which were seized by the police. He backed this up by producing written permission from one of the two tenants, William Robb (a merchant from Forth), which was dated 1894.

According to Johnston, he and Croft had shot the rabbits the previous night. They had left them, concealed, near the road, and gone into Bathgate to see if they could find a buyer. The next day they had returned and picked them up, at which point they had run into the police constable.

It was when William Robb took the witness-box that events took an unusual turn. He agreed that he had given Johnston permission to kill rabbits but not to shoot them, which he seemed to feel was a significant distinction, somewhat to the bafflement of the court. The paper records the following conversation as his questioning continued:

Sheriff Melville: What do you pay for the shooting?

The End Of The Century

William Robb: Am I entitled to tell that?

Sheriff: I think so. Why not?

Robb: Because it is my own affair.

Sheriff: Oh, very well; if you don't choose to tell.

Robb: I consider it is a quite private matter that, and I don't think I am entitled to tell my private affairs in a public way.

Sheriff: If you have nothing to hide, and are an honest man, you will tell us.

Robb: If you are saying I am bound to answer it I will answer the question, but I hold it is a quite private matter.

Sheriff: I think you are bound to tell us; your refusal is apt to leave a bad impression.

Robb: I will be guided by your lordship. If you say I should tell the rent I will do so.

Sheriff: Very well, tell us.

Robb: I pay £2 10s.

Questioned further, Robb confirmed that he had given permission to Johnston but stated that he did not know Croft. Clearly, the case against Johnston was over but that still left the co-accused. Another conversation is recorded.

Fiscal: I think we can still proceed against Croft. The rabbits were got in his possession.

Sheriff: If you give a man permission to kill rabbits, is he not entitled to get a man to carry them for him?

Fiscal: It's very suspicious.

Sheriff: I am very doubtful they got the rabbits at this place at all.

Fiscal:	There is no doubt they got them at another place altogether.
Sheriff:	However, there seems to be a doubt, and perhaps it is better to give them the benefit. In my own mind I have very little doubt that the rabbits were not got at this place.

Johnston and Croft were found not guilty, but that wasn't the end of matters. Robb returned to court to inquire whether he was to be paid his expenses as a witness. The Sheriff asked him if he really believed that Johnston had shot the rabbits on the ground he rented. Another exchange followed:

Robb:	I don't suppose one of them came from my ground. (Laughter in the court). If they got them there it is more than I could get. (More laughter).
Fiscal:	You might have told us that before.
Robb:	I told the police.

Robb continued to press for his expenses but the Sheriff was not minded to give them to him. Robb:

> 'left the Court protesting vigorously and threatening an action against the procuratorfiscal.'

I have not found any evidence that he took his threats any further!

The earlier offence was reported back in January of the same year in the Glasgow Herald's Crimes and Charges column. George Buchan, a labourer of no fixed residence, pled guilty to the charge of poaching on Broadlaw Farm in Uphall parish. His fine of 42s was in line with the fines being issued in the 1850s. However, he may well have had to take the alternative punishment of a month in jail. It is interesting to observe that the fine imposed was only a little less than the 50s rent which William Robb had eventually revealed he paid for (presumably) a year's shooting rights.

The third poaching case in this section came from the turn of the century and has echoes of the Johnston and Croft case. Whitburn Publican John Adam was accused of trespassing on Whitburn Farm in pursuit of game on 27th January 1900. Adam's defence was that he was in fact standing on the neighbouring land

The End Of The Century

at Whitedalehead Farm, for which he had a permit to shoot. However, he was found guilty because though standing where he was allowed, he was shooting into Whitburn Farm and sending in a dog to pick up the game. He was fined £2 with £2 11s 7d in expenses. Later that year, on 18 July, Adam took his case to the Appeal Court, lost and was fined a further seven guineas in expenses.

Fraud
Source:
Glasgow Herald, Tuesday 7th April 1896 and Monday 4th May 1896

Linlithgow Sheriff Court had two cases of fraudulent behaviour to consider in the Spring of 1896. The first of these brought an imaginative character before the Sheriff on Monday 6th April 1896.

The accused was Robert Hogg Lawson, a drover of no fixed abode, who had been making a nuisance of himself. The court heard that Lawson had gone to Robert Trew's house in Linlithgow Bridge a few days earlier, while Mr Trew was out at work as a fireman. He had spoken to Mrs Trew, saying that he had come to collect the shilling which her husband owed for two rabbits and a sheepskin he had sold him. In fact, Lawson did not even know Trew, but had gone to the works where he was employed and managed to find out his name and address. Mrs Trew was somewhat suspicious of this story but gave him the shilling. Emboldened, Lawson proceeded to tell Mrs Trew that he was a shepherd in the employment of Lord Rosebery (Prime Minister from 1894-5). He said that he urgently needed to send a telegram to his lordship. As this would cost a further 2 1/2 d he wondered if Mrs Trew would oblige him with the sum, as he had, unfortunately, come out without sufficient money. When Mrs Trew didn't like the sound of this and declined to give him any more cash, Lawson further embellished his story, saying that his brother was Lord Rosebery's gamekeeper and that he would ensure that she was sent two rabbits every week!

Eventually, Mrs Trew was able to get rid of Lawson and then contacted the police. Two constables were sent in search of him, locating and arresting him on the beach at Blackness. Further investigations found that Lawson was wanted in Dumbarton and had previous convictions for similar offences in Selkirk and Kirkcudbright.

In court, Lawson pled guilty, stating that it had all been done through drink. Sheriff Melville said that he could not accept that as an excuse and sentenced

The End Of The Century

Lawson to 40 days imprisonment.

The second case had its origins five days later, when James Watson Robertson began the path that was to bring him to the court at the start of May.

Robertson was an unemployed hammerman, or metal worker. On 11th April he went to the pay-office of the Seafield Oil Company in Bathgate and showed the clerks a document written by one of their staff, Walter Shanks, authorising them to hand over his pay to Robertson. On the strength of this, the clerk handed over £4 1s. It soon became clear that the document was a forgery.

On 1st May, Robertson repeated the trick, handing over a note purportedly written by Andrew Pettie to David Bogie at the pay-office of the Linlithgow Oil Company. He received Pettie's due wages of £1 10s and made off from the scene. However, the fraud came to light very quickly and the wronged man sought leave to pursue him. Pettie was furnished with a horse and trap and he and a group of men set off after Robertson. They caught up with him near Whitequarries, about five miles from Linlithgow. After a struggle they managed to detain him and transported him to the police station.

The Sheriff committed him to prison pending further investigation. The journalist reported suspicions that he had committed other crimes, and was wanted in Lanarkshire.

Both of these cases rather pale into insignificance compared to the item that followed Robertson's in the Glasgow Herald. This was a case from Ireland (which was still under British rule) of a man who had arrived in Lurgan, calling himself Captain Worth. He claimed that he had been sent to make arrangements for the stationing of 5,000 troops in the area for the following six months. He negotiated contracts with leading tradesmen in the area for the supply of goods and services, but was rumbled when someone thought to contact army HQ in Dublin.

A Day in the Sheriff Court in 1897
Source:
Glasgow Herald, Wednesday 13th January 1897

Linlithgow Sheriff Court seems to have been the place to be on Tuesday 12th January 1897. Not one, but three cases heard that day were reported in the Glasgow Herald's Crimes and Charges column.

The End Of The Century

The first concerned James McGregor, a vanman (presumably a van driver) from Glasgow. McGregor was charged with furious and reckless driving on New-Year's Day while under the influence of drink, proving that you don't need a motorised vehicle to be a drink driver. He pled guilty, explaining that he was visiting a friend in Broxburn, to whom the horse belonged, and who had invited him *'to give it a turn.'* He was fined £2 with the alternative of one month's imprisonment.

Next up was Queensferry shoemaker John White, aged 65. He apparently broke new ground, being the first person the court had tried under the Naval Discipline Act.

White had befriended a young lad who was a sailor, attached to the Training Ship Caledonia. The lad told White how unhappy he was and how hard life was on board. He said that he wanted to *'get away'*, by which he meant desert, but the only clothes he had were his naval uniform. He said that if he could get to Dunbar his brother would give him money.

White (described as *'the old man'*), took compassion (to use his own word) on the lad, and provided him with civilian clothes. He took the naval uniform and hid it under a bed, and cut up his leather boots for use in his daily trade.

The lad had managed to get as far as Edinburgh before the naval authorities laid hands on him and brought him back to his ship. In court, White admitted that he had done wrong. Taking into account his motives and admission, the Sheriff was lenient, letting him off with an admonishment.

The third case was brought against Jane McLean, from East Benhar. She was charged with a serious assault on an orphan girl on New Year's Day. McLean had found that some of her money was missing and believed that the girl had taken it. She questioned her but found the answers unsatisfactory, so she attacked the girl, knocking her unconscious!

It would seem that the girl was found in this state by someone else who then involved the police. McLean denied assault and Sheriff Melville asked her for an explanation for the girl's unconsciousness. McLean's defence was that, it being New Year's Day, the girl, who was thirteen years old, had got drunk. The Fiscal denied that this was the case, or the cause; presumably the police had brought in a doctor to examine her at the time. The Sheriff decided that:

'he could not do otherwise than send the accused to prison for 10 days.'

'Contempt of Court'
Source:
Glasgow Herald, Wednesday 25th August 1897

Matthew Campbell, a miner, fell foul of the law in the summer of 1897 and found himself before Sheriff-Substitute Hog in Linlithgow Sheriff Court.

Campbell had rented unfurnished accommodation in Uphall from John McKnight. Unfortunately, he had found himself in a position where he was unable to find work in the area and had therefore not kept up his rent payments. McKnight had taken him to court and had had his furniture sequestered against payment of the arrears. Campbell, meanwhile, had found work in Hamilton and had moved there. Having established himself in new accommodation, he returned to Uphall and took his furniture from his old house. He told the court that in doing this he did not think he had done anything wrong. The Sheriff disagreed! He told Campbell that the offence was not so much that he had not paid his rent, but that he had disobeyed an order of the court.

Short and Sad
Source:
Glasgow Herald, Tuesday 3rd May 1898

The Glasgow Herald contained a short and sad Linlithgowshire story on 3rd May 1898. Bo'ness parochial board made an application to Sheriff-Substitute Macleod at Linlithgow Sheriff Court for:

'an inquiry as to the sanity of the man James Gemmell, a pottery worker, Bo'ness.'

Gemmell had recently been arrested for the attempted murder of his wife. While in custody, he had shown signs of madness. A doctor examined him and wrote a medical certificate to have him temporarily confined to a lunatic asylum. Longer term certification required a formal enquiry ordered by the Sheriff Court; this was granted.

The End Of The Century

Lemonade Wars
Source:
The Scotsman, Wednesday 2nd August 1899
Glasgow Herald, Saturday 19th August 1899, Friday 29th December 1899 and
Thursday 11th January 1900

By the end of the nineteenth century many aspects of life had changed dramatically. One of the great steps forward delivered by the Industrial Revolution was mass production, which dramatically increased the range of goods available while driving down prices. This was made more profitable by improved transport links, which allowed goods to be readily available far from their place of production. These developments led to the emergence of brand names for the first time and 1897 the Merchandise Marks Act, which had been passed to help regulate this burgeoning area. All of these factors come together in a series of cases which relate to disputes in the burgeoning lemonade industry and the expanding operations of Falkirk manufacturer, Robert Barr.

Barr had founded his company in 1875 (the ancestor of Irn Bru producers A. G. Barr) and was trying to develop a distinctive brand. He did not want his customers to be in any doubt when they were drinking his products. In August 1899 he brought two actions against fellow aerated water manufacturers: William Sheal and John McIntosh, both of Bo'ness. Both were accused of contravening the 1897 Act. His anger had been aroused by finding that Sheal had been taking empty bottles with the Barr name and trademark on them and filling them with his own lemonade, while McIntosh had been reusing bottle-stoppers which he (Barr) had patented, and which had his trademark on them. Sheal came to court first, was found guilty and fined £1 and two guineas for expenses. When McIntosh's turn came it emerged, on the day of the trial, that he had agreed to settle out of court, paying Barr a sum of money for his expenses and making a donation to the funds of the Aerated Water Manufacturers' Association.

In November 1899, just three months later, Barr and McIntosh were back in court when Barr successfully brought an action for using bottles with the Barr name and trademark on them. Barr's joy, however, was short-lived as McIntosh continued to offend in this way. In late December Barr had evidence that McIntosh was continuing to use his empties. McIntosh pled guilty at yet another court hearing, but gave an interesting explanation. His main market was in the Uphall and Broxburn areas, where he was in competition not just with Barr but also with a number of Edinburgh companies. His, and the other companies, had

The End Of The Century

a practise of collecting empty bottles and refilling them, regardless of who had first used them. When he had started in business McInstosh had spent £1,700 on bottles, and since the court action in November he had needed to pay out £150 to replenish his stock. He was losing bottles because his own ones were being reused by the Edinburgh manufacturers, while he was not supposed to reuse the Barr's bottles, which were very common in Bo'ness. He told the court that if he was forced to stop using Barr's bottles he would go out of business.

The Sheriff responded that this did not justify him in using bottles with Barr's name on them. McIntosh was fined five guineas, with another five guineas in expenses, or 28 days imprisonment.

The very next month Robert Barr was back in Linlithgow Sheriff Court, pursuing a similar claim against another repeat offender, William Sheal. Sheal gave the same reasons as McIntosh, but with a similar lack of success. Sheal claimed that to carry on his business he needed something in the order of 24,000 to 36,000 bottles but actually owned a far smaller number, which shows the scale of operations that these companies ran.

In his fight to uphold his trademark and eliminate any suggestion of counterfeit goods, Barr repeatedly won the day in this very modern seeming case.

Double Trouble
Source:
Aberdeen Weekly Journal, Wednesday 9th August 1899

We will end with a case which resulted in some light entertainment at Linlithgow Sheriff Court on Thursday 3rd August 1899 when John Neally, a miner from Armadale appeared, charged with having committed a breach of the peace at Green Trees Cottages, Armadale.

Accompanying John Neally was his identical twin brother, George, wearing identical clothes. There was much amusement when one Crown witness after another, including the complainer and his wife, were unable to tell the two men apart. In the end, the Sheriff found himself unable see how he could safely convict John, so found him not guilty.

Endnotes

1. The Battle of Vitoria was a victory for Wellington's allied army against the French on 21st June 1813.
2. The Lord Justice Clerk was, and is, one of Scotland's most senior judges, second only to the Lord President of the Court of Session. From 1811 to 1841 the Lord Justice Clerk was Lord David Boyle, a former MP for Ayrshire and Solicitor General for Scotland.
3. Napoleon had been defeated in 1814 and exiled to the island of Elba. Three days after the publication of this article Napoleon escaped. Returning to France to retake power for a period now called the Hundred Days, before his final defeat at Waterloo.
4. Though we must not forget the ground-breaking assassination of the Regent Moray in Linlithgow High Street in 1570.
5. This might perhaps have been a mistake for Whitburn as Springfield farm lies between Whitburn and Armadale.
6. To add to the distress of this girl, it was not, apparently, until the trial that she discovered that Peter McLean was not, in fact, her father.
7. This gentleman, in a connection back to the previous case, was a solicitor employed by the late Mr Alexander Hedderwick.
8. The Parks Regulation Act, 1872, regulated the use and management of royal parks and gardens.
9. 'Shooting tenants' were men who had paid for the shooting right on the farms.

POSTSCRIPT

The nineteenth century had seen great changes in the way the people of Britain lived their lives and the way they dealt with those who broke the law. In reading through these cases there can be little doubt that class and background mattered enormously in the outcome of trials. When it came to motivation, the higher ranks of society were given the benefit of the doubt. On the other hand, when it was clear that those elements of society which should be setting an example to the rest had fallen from grace there was a deep sense of hurt and disappointment.

Though the lives of the inhabitants of the country changed in many ways, their nature did not. The people of 1900 had the same human frailties as those of 1800, 1000, 2000, or any other year. Some themes recur throughout the century, and they will come as no surprise to the reader. Alcohol and poverty were underlying causes in many offences, especially of assault and petty theft. Visit any court in Scotland, or any Accident and Emergency Department on a Saturday night today and the same themes still come through. One major difference is that there seems to have been a tolerance in the nineteenth century of a degree of domestic violence which we find completely unacceptable today, with the authorities only taking an interest when matters got seriously out of hand.

If the make-up of the people of Scotland is much the same as it always was, what has developed over time is society's attitude to these frailties, what it is prepared to accept, how it attempts to prevent other occurrences, and how it deals with the perpetrators. Methods of punishment changed through the nineteenth century, as the state developed the capacity to hold people for longer custodial sentences. The eye-watering harshness of the punishments meted out in the early decades gradually gave way to more moderate, though still severe, sentences. This is especially the case for crimes against property.

Within the ever more centralised and standardised prison system a long running experiment was tried in hard-line deterrence which failed to demonstrate a positive impact on the crime figures. With the 1895 Gladstone Report, and the 1898 Prison Act, a new experiment began in which the objective was not just to punish, but also to make the individual better able to contribute to society once his or her sentence was over.

The cases in the 1880s and 90s show that by the end of the century people, whether they were husbands, wives, parents, workmates or employers were considered to have a greater degree of responsibility to those around them and the courts were less prepared to see harm done to one person through the neglect or carelessness of others.

The period also saw the development not just of national but global news with people on the far side of the world reading stories about the misdeeds, or at least the more quirky ones, of Linlithgowshire residents.

Crimes and their Punishments

The following table lists the crimes recorded in this book where the accused were found guilty and a punishment was recorded.

Year of Trial	Name	Occupation, If Stated	Crime Convicted Of	Punishment
1803	John Berry	-	Stealing from the post	Banishment for 7 years
1803	James Taylor	-	Stealing butter and cheese	Banishment for life
1803	Mrs Kilpatrick Mrs Henderson	Lodging house keepers	Putting a dying girl out on to the streets	Fined 2 guineas Banished from Glasgow for 3 years
1807	Richard Hamilton	Miner	Hamesucken and culpable homicide	Transportation for life
1807	Thomas Smith George Stevenson	Horse breaker Cabinet maker	Theft of horses	Hanged
1808	John Grierson	Grain measurer	Theft of grain	1 month in prison and £10 fine
1808	James Galbreath Janet Cowie William Brown John Glass Walter Pollock Thomas Carlaw Peter Henderson	Carters	Theft of grain	1 week in prison and 2 guineas fine
1815	Thomas Frew (sen)	Miner	Assault and robbery	1 year in prison
1815	Alexander Cuming	Miner	Assault and robbery	Transportation for 7 years

165

Year of Trial	Name	Occupation, If Stated	Crime Convicted Of	Punishment
1815	James Miller George Paterson William Burns	Calico printers	Unlawful combination	Outlawed for non-appearance
1815	John Murdoch	Wright, ex army	Murder	Hanged
1818	Robert Tenant	Former mill worker	Theft of oatmeal	Transportation for 14 years
1818	Alexander Spence Peter Liddle	Apprentice shoemakers	Housebreaking and theft	Outlawed for non-appearance
1819	Robert Millar	Weaver	Insulting a Justice of the Peace	Fined £5 plus expenses
1819	Unknown	Baker's lad	Walking on the pavement with a basket of bread on his head, and refusing to go onto the road when ordered by a policeman	Fined 10s
1819	John Duncan	Carter	Allowing his horse, pulling a loaded cart, to wander unattended through the streets	Fined £1
1819	Robert Symington Robert Duff	-	Stealing a bag of potatoes	30 days in prison
1819	Ralph Woodness	-	Stealing from a shop cloth and other goods worth c£350	Hanged
1819	James Whiteford	Shoemaker	Breaking and entering, assault and theft of c£11, a bottle of whisky and a loaf	Hanged
1819	Richard Smith	-	Assaulting young girls	Transportation for 7 years

Year of Trial	Name	Occupation, If Stated	Crime Convicted Of	Punishment
1825	James Wright	Canal boatman	Stealing hay from a field	6 weeks in prison
1828	William Elder	-	Night poaching	6 weeks in prison, £10 fine and £10 surety
1829	Helen Dot	-	Theft of several items from a cart and of a gown	Transportation for 7 years
1829	George Baird	Gardener	Housebreaking	Transportation for 14 years
1836	Ann Watson	-	Forging money	Transportation for life
1838	Margaret Blackhall	-	Stealing 3 cast-iron window sash weights	Transportation for 7 years
1838	Alexander McKay	-	Stealing from a house a pair of gloves, a snuff-box and a brooch	Transportation for 7 years
1838	John Spears	-	Stealing a bible	Transportation for 7 years
1838	John McDonald George Smith Archibald Richmond	-	Stealing from a shop two powder flasks, eight guns and a pistol	Transportation for 7 years
1838	George Allan	-	Four counts of housebreaking, theft of 400 lbs of sugar, 22 yards of cloth and a large quantity of whisky	Transportation for 14 years
1838	Luigi Deschalzo	-	Falsehood and forgery	Outlawed for non-appearance

167

Year of Trial	Name	Occupation, If Stated	Crime Convicted Of	Punishment
1838	Charles Stewart Arthur Corner John Bruce James Blair	- - - House servant	Abduction, assault and robbery	Transportation for 14 years
1840	James Dalrymple	Estate worker	Murder	Transportation for life
1842	Dundas McRiner	Labourer	Culpable homicide	Transportation for 21 years
1842	Margaret Beattie	-	3 charges of theft	Transportation for 7 years
1842	William Sommerville	Shoemaker	Stealing a pair of women's boots	18 months in prison
1842	Thomas Flight	Nailer	Stole 2 sheep and a cart	18 months in prison
1842	Alexander Cummings	Flesher	Assisted Thomas Flight	9 months in prison
1842	Margaret Anderson Elizabeth Stewart	-	Stole 10 shirts and a silk handkerchief	Transportation for 7 years
1846	Catherine McGavin	-	Culpable homicide	Transportation for 7 years
1846	John Scott	Limeburner	Forging £50 bill of exchange	Transportation for 7 years
1846	Euphemia Haxton	Servant	Stealing 60 towels, 49 table cloths, 24 pairs of linen sheets, and a great many similar articles	Transportation for 7 years
1849	Robert Brownlee James Mossman jnr James Lind	Mason Wright Shoemaker	Poaching	Fined £1 and expenses of 5s 4d
1849	James Hughes	-	Poaching	Fined 10s and expenses of 14s 6d
1849	Alexander Jack Henry Marshall	Mason Wright Shoemaker	Poaching	Fined 10s and expenses of 7s 6d

Year of Trial	Name	Occupation, If Stated	Crime Convicted Of	Punishment
1849	John Thomson	Publican	Entertaining people in his house at unseasonable hours	Fined 25s and expenses of 12s 6d
1849	Henry Peddie	Publican	Entertaining people in his house at unseasonable hours	Fined 25s and expenses of 9s 6d
1850	Sir John Dick Lauder	-	Assault	Fined £10
1851	William Graham	-	Assault	Outlawed for non-appearance
1857	William Wallace	Publican	Entertaining people in his house at unseasonable hours	Fined 25s and expenses
1857	John Anderson	Publican	Entertaining people in his house at unseasonable hours	Fined 25s and expenses
1857	Janet Bryson	Publican	Entertaining people in his house at unseasonable hours	Fined 25s and expenses
1857	Peter McLean	Miner	Murder	Hanged
1857	William Mansfield	Miner	Assault	2 years hard labour
1858	Robert Aitken Thomas Ramage William Gillespie John Bellany	Miners	Poaching	Fined £2 and expenses of 6s 6d
1858	James Murdoch	Miner	Poaching	Fined 21s and expenses of 19s

Year of Trial	Name	Occupation, If Stated	Crime Convicted Of	Punishment
1858	James Pringle	Engine-keeper	Poaching	Fined 32s and expenses of 14s 6d
1858	William Carmichael	Miner	Poaching	Fined 26s and expenses of 14s
1858	Peter Fenwick	Miner	Trespassing	Fined £2 and expenses
1860	Graham Stewart	-	Selling spirits without a license	Fined £25
1860	James McIver	At Iron Works	Alimony following legal separation on grounds of repeated physical abuse	Alimony of £26 granted
1861	Bridget Kelly	-	Assault	6 months in prison
1862	William McKinlay	-	Missed training in militia for 4 years	2 months in prison and a fine of £2
1862	Bernard Crawson	Soldier	Enlisting while a member of the militia	1 month in prison
1862	Mary Murdoch	-	Stealing clothes from a locked drawer	6 months in prison
1863	Edinburgh and Glasgow Railway	-	Responsible for death of son	£1,750 (to Joanna Hedderwick)
1863	Edinburgh and Glasgow Railway	-	Responsible for personal injuries	£2,000 (to Mr Shaw)
1863	Edinburgh and Glasgow Railway	-	Responsible for personal injuries	£3,000 (to Henry Welsh)
1863	Edinburgh and Glasgow Railway	-	Responsible for personal injuries	£1,800 (to Mr Elder)
1863	Edinburgh and Glasgow Railway	-	Responsible for death of unborn child	£250 plus £150 costs (to Eliza Gibb)

Year of Trial	Name	Occupation, If Stated	Crime Convicted Of	Punishment
1866	Alex Seton	Farmer and Deputy Lieutenant of Linlithgowshire	Transporting 39 sheep during a period of livestock movement restrictions	Fined £5 plus costs
1866	George Somerville	Farmer	Failing to dispose properly of infected animal carcasses	Fined £25 plus costs
1866	George Tait	Flesher	Transporting 6 sheep during a period of livestock movement restrictions	Fined £2 plus unrecorded costs
1866	D Walkinshaw	Flesher	Transporting 'some fat sheep' during a period of livestock movement restrictions	Fined £5 plus costs
1866	Thomas Borthwick	Flesher	Transporting a bullock during a period of livestock movement restrictions	Fined £5 plus costs
1866	James Williamson	Basket maker	Culpable homicide	15 years penal servitude
1872	John McLure	Cashier	Embezzlement	5 years penal servitude
1872	William Bryce Hugh Binnie	Carters	Toll evasion	1 month in prison
1872	Thomas West	Shoemaker	Assault	7 years penal servitude
1873	George Farrie	Miner	Culpable homicide	15 years penal servitude
1875	Thomas Morris	Miner	Breach of promise	£50 plus costs
1876	-	Butler	Theft of leftover rabbit and bacon cutlets	A ticking off

Year of Trial	Name	Occupation, If Stated	Crime Convicted Of	Punishment
1877	David Hill	Grocer, spirit dealer and magistrate	Breach of the peace	Fined £5
1877	Peter Pickard	Shoemaker and town councillor	Breach of the peace	Fined £2 or 14 days in prison
1877	Peter Pickard	Shoemaker and town councillor	Breach of the peace	Fined £1 or 14 days in prison
1877	John Black	Labourer	Breach of the peace	Fined 15s or 10 days in prison
1877	Mary Crichton	-	Infanticide	5 years penal servitude
1877	Maggie Mutch	-	Infanticide	5 years penal servitude
1883	Frances Kane	-	Culpable homicide	5 years penal servitude
1883	Samuel Gibson	Chemist Shop Owner	Multiple assaults	60 days in prison
1886	William Murray Alexander Barras	Miners	Culpable homicide	6 months in prison
1891	David Nicolson	-	Assault	Bound over to keep the peace
1892	Hugh Meechan Henry Bryce	- -	Pulling feather out of a peacock's tail	1 week in prison 6 strips of a birch rod
1892	James Malley	Miner	Having cruelly ill-treated and neglected his 4 year old child by failing to provide him with food sufficient and proper for his nourishment, and by abusing him repeatedly with a poker and a whip	2 months hard labour

Year of Trial	Name	Occupation, If Stated	Crime Convicted Of	Punishment
1892	Eliza Armstrong	-	Murder of her child	Detained indefinitely
1892	William Watt	Shoemaker	Stealing a bottle of whisky from a drunk	1 month in prison
1893	James Black	Labourer	Assaulting a Police Officer	60 days hard lbour
1893	Allan Nicol	Labourer	Assault	60 days in prison
1893	Hermand Oil Company	-	Sued for negligence leading to the death of a child	£100 compensation awarded
1894	Alexander Mather	Publican	Selling watered down whisky	Fined £2
1894	George Gardner	Dairyman	Selling low fat milk	Fined 3 guineas
1895	William Horsburgh John McNaught	Soldiers	Stealing apples	Admonished
1896	George Buchan	Labourer	Poaching	Fined 42s or 1 month is prison
1896	John Green	-	Wife-beating	Fined 30s or 30 days in prison
1896	Robert Hogg Lawson	Drover	Fraud	40 days in prison
1897	John Wood	Labourer	Child neglect	Admonished
1897	James McGregor	Van driver	Reckless driving while under the influence	Fined £2 or 1 month in prison
1897	John White	Shoemaker	Assisting a Royal Navy sailor to desert	Admonished
1897	Jane McLean	-	Assault	10 days in prison
1898	George Burden	Miner	Possession of matches in a pit	Fined 5s or 3 days in prison

Year of Trial	Name	Occupation, If Stated	Crime Convicted Of	Punishment
1898	Robert Rooney	Miner	Smoking in restricted area beside a pit	Fined 5s or 3 days in prison
1899	Mining Company		Sued for negligence leading to the death of a husband	£234 compensation awarded
1899	William Sheal	Lemonade manufacturer	Using bottles trademarked by another manufacturer	Fined £1 and 2 guineas in expenses
1899	John McIntosh	Lemonade manufacturer	Repeatedly using bottles trademarked by another manufacturer	Fined 5 guineas plus 5 guineas expenses or 28 days in prison
1900	John Adam	Publican	Poaching	Fined £2 plus expenses of £2 11s 7d (later lost appeal and was fined a further 7 guineas in expenses)

INDEX

Adam, John 155-6
Adie, Mr 111
Ainslie, Mrs 21
Airdrie 21, 33
Aitken, James (1) 20-2
Aitken, James (2) 105
Aitken, Robert 133
Aitken, Robert 77
Alexander, William 143
Allan, George 54
Anderson, Adam 88, 90-1
Anderson, Jean 23-4
Anderson, John (1) 78
Anderson, John (2) 149
Anderson, Margaret 72
Anderson, Mr 135-6
Anderson, Robert 127
Andrews, Sarah 41
Arbuckle, Mr 30-2
Arden 118
Ardmillan, Lord 110
Armadale 21, 77, 124, 125-6, 149, 161
Armadale Inn 21
Armstrong, Eliza 146-7
Australia 10, 11, 102, 125
Ayr 151
Baillie, Sir William 76, 77
Baird, Dr 59-60, 75, 123-4
Baird, George 42
Balerno 37
Barbauchlaw Row 77
Barclay, Mr 72-3
Barr, Robert 160-1
Barras, Alexander 142
Bartholomew, John 41

Bassett, William Jesse 84, 88-91
Bathgate 9, 21, 22, 27, 34-5, 54, 68, 69-70, 78-9, 92-95, 105-6, 124, 125-6, 151, 153, 157
Bauchop, Jenny 21
Beattie, Margaret 71-2
Beattie, Mr 133
Bell, Reverend Doctor 97
Bellany, John 77
Bennett, Samuel 123
Benny, Alex 51-2
Berry, John 16
Berry, Thomas 54
Beveridge, Mr 15
Binnie, Hugh 118-9
Black, George 128
Black, Hector 55
Black, James (1) 77
Black, James (2) 149
Black, John 128
Black, William 26-8
Blackburn 78, 144
Blackhall, Margaret 54
Blackness Castle & village 152, 156
Blair, John 55
Blair, Sheriff 142
Bo'ness (inc Borrowstouness and other variations) 9, 16, 17-8, 19, 42, 68, 76, 78, 99, 139-42, 146, 148, 151, 159, 160-1
Boarstane 54
Bogie, David 157
Bonnytoun Distillery 18-19
Borrowsoun-mains 46-7
Borthwick, Thomas 115
Bourhill, Euphemia 79-80

Brackenbury, Thomas 147-8
Breich 150
Bridewell Prison 24, 35
Bridge of Allan 113
Bridgehouse Castle 79
Bristol 126
Broadlaw Farm 155
Brodie, John 123
Broglan, Constable 99
Brounlie, Mary 17
Brown, James 45-6
Brown, John 145
Brown, John 29
Brown, Robert 15-16
Brown, William 19
Brownieside 118
Brownlee, Robert 76
Broxburn 147, 168, 160
Bruce, John 55
Bryce, Henry 145
Bryce, William 118-9
Bryson, Janet (Rankine) 78
Buchan, George 155
Bullock, Alexander 44
Burden, George 151
Burghmuir 57-60
Burns, William 25
Byers, Peter 143
Cairn, Mary 124
Calcraft, Mr 97-8
Campbell, John, 52
Campbell, Matthew 159
Campbell, William 52
Campsie, Mr 49-53
Carlaw, Thomas 19
Carmichael, William 77
Carniehead, Linlithgow 92
Carr, Sergeant 78
Causewayhead 80
Cay, Sheriff 81, 107

Chalmers, Robert 149
Champany 56, 58
Clark, James 15-16
Clark, Police Constable 126
Cleghorn, Mr 85, 88, 90
Coatbridge 151
Cochrane, Mr 151
Colquhoun, Chief Constable Adam 112
Cook, Joseph 147-8
Corbet, James Esq. 35
Corkle, John 92
Corner, Arthur 55
Cowdenhead 77
Cowie, Janet 19
Crawford, Mr 46
Crawson, Bernard 105
Creely, Mary (Kane, or Cain) 139-40
Crichton, Margaret 129
Crichton, Sheriff 142
Croft, Francis 153-5
Cross Keys Inn, Falkirk 44
Crossgates 144
Cuddie, Mr 78-9
Cuming, Alexander 23-4
Cummings, Alexander 72
Cunningham, Anne 121-2
Cuthbert, Mr (see Cuddie)
Dalkeith 44, 54, 115
Dalmeny Park 43
Dalrymple, Alexander 56-62
Dalrymple, James 55-62
Dalrymple, John 59
Dalrymple, William 58
Dalyell, Sir James 60
Dawson, Adam (1) 19
Dawson, Adam (2) 49-53, 74-6
Dawson, Adam (3) 107, 132-3
Dawson, John 49-53, 74-6
Deans, Adam 130-1
Deas, Lord 129

Dechmont 21-3
Deschalzo, Luigi 54-5
Devellin, Patrick 94
Devine, Peter 144
Dick Lauder, Sir John 82-91
Don, Sir William H 81-8
Dott, Helen 41-2
Dougal, George 133, 144
Duff, James 35
Duff, Mungo 80
Dumbarton 156
Duncan, Henry 37-8
Duncan, John 35
Duncan, Mary 37
Dunlop, Mr 111
Dunlop, Thomas 26-8
Durhamtown 93-5
Durie, Messers John & Co. 20-1
East Benhar, Whitburn 146, 158
Easter Whitburn 45
Ecclesmachan 120
Edgar, Andrew 36-7
Edinburgh 15-16, 19-22, 24, 28, 30, 34-5, 36, 38, 40, 41, 44, 50, 54, 80, 81, 84, 88-91, 96, 97, 98, 103, 107-9, 112, 115, 118, 119, 133, 134, 135, 142, 158, 160-1
Edinburgh and Glasgow Railway (and Company) 40, 55-6, 62, 68, 81, 89-90, 106-14, 132
Elder, Mr 114
Elder, William 43
Falkirk 41, 44, 79, 80, 93, 107, 112, 142, 150, 160
Farrie, Catherine 120-3
Farrie, George 120-3
Fenwick, Peter 77
Flight, Thomas 72
Flint, Jane 58
Forfar 134
Forrest, James 26-8

Forrester, Mrs 21
Forrester, William 42-3
Forth 153
Fraser, Alexander (1) 56-7
Fraser, Alexander (2) 78-9
Fraser, Donald 55-62
Frew, Elizabeth 23-4
Frew, Thomas (Jnr) 23-4
Frew, Thomas (Snr) 23-4
Galbreath, James 19
Gallacher, William 105-6
Gardner, George 148
Gay, Thomas 104
Geddes, John 26-8
Gemmell, James 159
Gibb, Eliza 114
Gibson Maitland, Sir Alexander 82-4
Gibson, Samuel 140-1
Gifford, John 58-9
Gifford, Thomas 58
Gillespie, William 77
Gillon, W. D. 53
Glasgow 15, 16, 17, 19-23, 28-9, 33, 36-7, 40, 44, 82, 91, 107-9, 158
Glass, John 19
Glendinning, William 18
Gorebridge 115
Grady, Mrs 119-20
Graham, John 150-1
Graham, Marion 42
Graham, William 92
Grangepans 17, 23, 42, 148
Grant, John 23-4
Gray, David (1) 20-2
Gray, David (2) 34
Gray, James 80
Green, John 148-9
Greendykes 41
Greenfield, Andrew 41
Greenhorn's Inn 26-7

177

Grierson, John 19
Haddington 104, 124
Hamilton, James 19-23
Hamilton, John 150
Hamilton, Richard 18-19
Hamilton, William 150
Handyside, Dr 113
Handyside, Mr 60
Hardie, Mr 133
Harkin, James 144
Harkin, Mrs 144
Hastion, John 58
Haxton, Euphemia 71
Hedderwick, Alexander 112
Hedderwick, Joanna 111-3
Heltzer, Lucy 145
Henderson, Mrs 17
Henderson, Peter 19
Hermand Oil Company 150
Hermiston 80
Heugh, Tom 133, 134
Hill, Alexander 23
Hill, David 127-8
Hill, Mr 63-5
Hillhouse 71
Home, Sheriff-Substitute 119
Hopetoun Woods 36-7
Horsburgh, Private William 152
Hughes, James 76
Hunter, Thomas (Jnr) 138
Hutton, Mr 133
Inverness 142
Irvine 148
Jack, Alexander 76
Jamieson, Mr (1) 111
Jamieson, Mr (2) 133
Jamieson, Mr (3) 134
Jane Pritchard (Black) 128
Jeffray, John 54
Jeffrey, Mr 24

Jerviswoode, Lord 110
Johnston, David 153-5
Kane, Francis (Cain) 139-40
Kelly, Bridget 103-4
Kennedy, Alexander 52
Kennedy, Lord Gilbert 82-4
Ker, Mr 15
Kerr, Mary 93, 95
Kerr, Sergeant 93, 95
Kettlestone 55
Kilpatrick, Mrs 17
Kinneil Estate 76
Kinneil Iron Works 99
Kirk of Shotts 33
Kirkcudbright 156
Kirkliston 118, 149,
Lanark 142
Lang, Archibald 130
Lang, Helen 130
Lang, Robert Jack 41
Langrig 26
Langrighead 25-30
Latham, John 89-91, 109-11
Law, James 133
Lawson, Robert Hogg 156
Leith 20-22
Liddle, Peter 34
Lind, James 76
Lindsay, John 26, 29
Linlithgow and Stirlingshire Hunt 81
Linlithgow Burgh Halls (Tolbooth) 9, 23, 97, 130
Linlithgow Canal basin 55
Linlithgow County Buildings 96-7
Linlithgow High Street 97, 130, 140-1
Linlithgow Loch 23-4, 132-6
Linlithgow Oil Company 157
Linlithgow Parish Funeral Society 130-1
Linlithgow Railway Station 81-84
Linlithgow Town Drummer 36, 133, 134

Liston, Thomas Esq. 62
Livingstone Mill 18
Lizars, Professor 82-4
Lothian, John 21
Love, Peter 45-6
Lurgan 157
Macaulay, Dennis 151
Macaulay, Jane 152
Macaulay, Sarah (Bonar) 151-2
MacDonald, James F. 150
Macdonald, Sheriff 51
Mackenzie, Reverend Kenneth 99
Mackie, Joseph 133-6
Macleod, Sheriff-Substitute 159
Maconochie, J. A. Esq. 49-53
Maitland, Mr 75
Malley, Alexander 146
Malley, James 146
Manchester 146
Mansfield, William 93-7
Marshall, Henry 76
Mason, William 42-3
Masterton, Hugh 82-3
Mather, Alexander 148
Maxwell, John 93-5
Maxwell, Thomas 93-5
McAlpine, Councillor 133-4
McArdel, Philip 126
McArthur, Alexander 55
McArtney, the Reverend 126
McBrierty, Charles 23-4
McDonald, John 54
McGavin, Catherine (Fairley) 70-1
McGlachan, Edward 93, 94
McGregor, James 158
McIntosh, John 160-1
McIver, Francis 98-9
McIver, James 98-9
McKay, Alexander 54
McKinlay, William 104-5

McKnight, John 159
McLean, Christina 93-7
McLean, Jane 158
McLean, Peter 93-8
McLellan, Daniel 21-2
McLure, John 117, 118
McMullen, Neil 93, 94-5
McNaught, Private John 152
McNeil, Mr 33
McNeill, James 73-4
McRiner, Dundas 69-70
McRiner, Marion (Wardrop) 69-60
Meadowbank, Lord 61-2
Medwyn, Lord 62
Meechan, Hugh 145
Meek, Mr 133
Meikle, Archibald 32-3
Meikle, John 19
Meikle, Robert 52
Melville, Sheriff 146, 148, 149, 150, 153-5
Mickel, Mr 133
Mid Calder 80
Millar, Robert 34-5
Miller, Baillie 148
Miller, James 25
Miller, Peter 128, 133
Moncrieff, Lord 61-2, 70,
Monro, Mr 125-6
Morris, Thomas 124
Morritt, Mr 82-4
Mossend, West Calder 150
Mossman, James (jnr) 76
Muir of Ord 142
Muir, Colin 150-1
Munro, Dr 30
Murdoch, James (1) 25-30
Murdoch, James (2) 77
Murdoch, John 26-30
Murdoch, Mary (McKenna, Morton or

McCann) 106
Murray, Mr 23
Murray, William 142
Mutch, Maggie 129
Napier, George Esq. 60
Neally, George 161
Neally, John (1) 103
Neally, John (2) 161
Neaves, Mr 85, 88, 90
Neil, Archibald 113
New Deer 129
New Mains Farm 115
New Zealand 8, 125-6
Newhouse Farm 77
Newton, George 108-9, 112, 113
Nichol, James 59
Nicol, Allan 148
Nicol, William 74-6
Nicolson, David 145
Niddry Mains Farm 76
Nimmo, Elizabeth 34
North British Railway Company 114, 150
Northridge 77
Noval, James 29
Over Hillhouse Farm 77
Parkfoot 115
Paterson, George 25
Pathfoot 115
Pattinson, Mr 74-5
Peddie, Henry 78
Perth 44, 68, 107, 113
Pettie, Andrew 157
Pickard, Peter 127-8
Polkemmet 33, 76, 77, 118
Pollan, James 93, 94-5
Pollock, Alexander 35-6
Pollock, Walter 19
Portobello 44
Pouflats 76
Preston Farm 76, 115

Prestonmains Farm 115
Pringle, James 77
Puncheonlaw 43
Purdie, Dr Robert 28
Queensferry 9, 30, 35-6, 41, 55, 127-8, 158
Rae, Elizabeth 141
Rae, Mr 141
Ramage, Thomas 77
Ramsay, Mr (1) 82-4
Ramsay, Mr (2) 135
Ratho 80, 84, 88, 107, 115
Richmond, Archibald 54
Robb, John 26-8
Robb, William 153-5
Robertson, James Watson 157
Robertson, Pat 61
Robertson, Rev. Mr 18
Romilly, Sir Samuel 31
Ronaldson, Mr 15
Rooney, Robert 151
Ross, Mr 46
Ross, Robert 56-7
Russel, Messers & Son 93
Russell, Walter 141-2
Rutherford, Constable 99
Salvation Army 145
Sangster, Constable 122
Scotland, Isabella 146
Scott, John 71
Scottish Widows 114
Seafield Oil Company 157
Selkirk 156
Seton, Alexander Esq. 76, 115
Shanks, Walter 157
Shaw, Mr 114
Sheal, William 160-1
Shillinglaw, Major 28
Shotts Iron Company 118
Simpson, John 42-3
Sinclair, Mr & Mrs 36-7

Skinner, Dr 121-2
Skipton 147
Smith, George 54
Smith, John 23
Smith, Richard 36-7
Smith, Thomas 18
Snab Pit, Bo'ness 151
Snadden, James 99
Somerville, George 115
Sommerville, William 72
South Queensferry (see Queensferry)
Spears, John 54
Spence, Alexander 34
Springfield Farm, Linlithgow 129
Springfield Farm, Whitburn 77
St Magdalene's Distillery 19, 49-53, 74-76, 147
Star and Garter, Linlithgow 81, 84, 136
Stevenson, George 18
Stevenson, James 149
Stewart, Captain Robert 126-7
Stewart, Captain Stirling 82-4
Stewart, Charles 55
Stewart, Elizabeth 72
Stewart, Graham 79
Stewart, James 17
Stewart, Katherine 17-18
Stewart, Mr 89
Stewart, William 22
Syme, Professor 114
Symington, Robert 35
Tait, George 115
Taylor, James 16
Taylor, William 30
Temple Blair, Henry Esq. 104-5
Tenant, Robert 32-3
Thomson, Dr Andrew 60
Thomson, George 142
Thomson, James Boyd 110-1
Thomson, John 78

Torbanehill Mains Farm 77
Torphichen 79
Tough, Adam 20-2
Trew, Mrs 156
Trew, Robert 156
Turnbull, James 80
Turpie, Robert 49
Tyler, Captain 108-10
Union Canal 18, 40, 41, 43, 49, 55, 79-80, 102
Uphall 20, 33, 41, 69, 70-71, 76, 119-122, 144, 151, 155, 159, 160
Waldie, George 133
Walker, Archibald 32-3
Walker, Janet (Cunningham) 116, 130-1
Walker, Mr 44
Walker, William 130-1
Walkinshaw, Mr D. 115
Wallace, William 78
Watson, Anne 48
Watson, Messers John & Sons 125
Watson, Mr 32
Watt, James 21-2
Watt, William & Son 123
Watt, William 147
Weir, Dr James 28
Welsh, Henry 111, 113-4
West Binny 32
West Calder 143, 150
West, Thomas 123-4
Whitburn 25-30, 45-6, 104, 143, 146, 155-6
Whitburn Farm 155
White, John 158
White, Mr 23
Whitedalehead Farm 156
Whiteford, James 36-8
Whitequarries 157
Witham (possibly an error for Whitburn) 77

Whitham 77
Williamson, Isabella 119-20
Williamson, James 119-20
Williamson, Mr 49, 52-3
Winchburgh 47, 76, 84, 106-14
Wood, John 57
Woodhead Row 77
Woodness, Ralph 36-7
Woods, John 147
Worth, Captain 157
Wotherspoon, Mr 133
Wright, James 41
Yorkston, George 65
Youden, Stephen 49-53
Young, Mr 82-4

Printed in Poland
by Amazon Fulfillment
Poland Sp. z o.o., Wrocław